The Lay-Centered Church

Theology and Spirituality

The Lay-Centered Church

Theology and Spirituality

Leonard Doohan

WINSTON PRESS

Other books by the author:
Luke: The Perennial Spirituality
John Paul II and the Laity: The Early Years

Cover design: Terry Dugan

Library of Congress Catalog Card Number: 83-51391

ISBN: 0-86683-808-2

Printed in the United States of America

5   4   3   2

Winston Press, Inc.
430 Oak Grove
Minneapolis, Minnesota 55403

*I dedicate this work to
my parents, Eva and John Doohan,
and to my wife's parents,
Cecelia and Julius Liona,
four laity who have truly lived
as "called and gifted."*

Acknowledgment is gratefully given for the following:

Karl Rahner for permission to quote from his open letter to Cardinal Razinger as reprinted in the *National Catholic Reporter*, 23 Nov. 1979, p. 1.

Document on the Church, 7:8; 9:6; 13:3; 31:1; 32:2; 36; Document on the Church Today 31:4; 40:4; Document on Laity 4:7; 5; 7:1; Document on Missions 11:1; 21:1; Document on Education 3:1—reprinted from *Documents of Vatican II*, Walter M. Abbott, S.J., general editor, © 1966. By permission of New Century Publishers, Inc., Piscataway, N.J. 08854.

Excerpts from *To Build and Be Church* copyright © 1979 by Brian T. Joyce, "Ministers and Ministries," p. 23; Robert Kinast, "The Laity: A Theological Perspective," p. 7; Thomas Allen, "Diaconate, Catechumenate, Lay Ministry," p. 25, are used with permission.

A. Jones, "Bishops: Laity Invisible to the World," which appeared in March 30, 1979, issue of the *National Catholic Reporter*; reprinted by permission of the *National Catholic Reporter*, P. O. Box 281, Kansas City, Mo. 64141.

Chapter 1 of this book is an expanded version of an article that first appeared in *Communio: International Catholic Review* 7 (1980): 225-242. That material is used here with permission of *Communio*.

I also wish to gratefully acknowledge the comments of colleagues and friends who reviewed the manuscript: Father Charles Skok, Kathy and Mitch Finley, Maureen and Joe Schneider. My special thanks go to Ms. Patricia O'Brien, for her help in the early stages of preparing the manuscript, and to Cyril A. Reilly of Winston Press for his careful editing.

Abbreviations of the titles of the documents of Vatican II:

B	*Bishops* (Decree on the Bishop's Pastoral Office in the Church)
C	*Church* (Dogmatic Constitution on the Church)
CO	*Communications* (Decree on the Instruments of Social Communication)
CT	*Church Today* (Pastoral Constitution on the Church in the Modern World)
E	*Ecumenism* (Decree on Ecumenism)
EC	*Eastern Churches* (Decree on Eastern Catholic Churches)
Ed	*Education* (Declaration on Christian Education)
L	*Laity* (Decree on the Apostolate of the Laity)
Lit	*Liturgy* (Constitution on the Sacred Liturgy)
M	*Missions* (Decree on the Church's Missionary Activity)
NC	*Non-Christians* (Declaration on the Relationship of the Church to Non-Christian Religions)
P	*Priests* (Decree on the Ministry and Life of Priests)
PF	*Priestly Formation* (Decree on Priestly Formation)
R	*Revelation* (Dogmatic Constitution on Divine Revelation)
RF	*Religious Freedom* (Declaration on Religious Freedom)
RL	*Religious Life* (Decree on the Appropriate Renewal of the Religious Life)

Contents

Preface

Perhaps for the first time in history we are ready for a lay-centered Church. Never before have there been so many educated and committed laity. In fact, for the first time in history there are in the Church today more theologically trained laity than priests or religious. The same is true numerically of dedicated and involved laity.

The ability of the Church to carry on its mission is increasingly dependent on laity. Priests and religious are discerning that they can best use their time and training by facilitating in laity a sense of Church and a commitment to ministry. They also see that giving spiritual direction to the laity is more important than administering buildings and finance. Leadership training and religious education for laity need to take precedence over attempts to build community through such activities as fund-raising events.

In short, we see the lay-centered Church of tomorrow already taking shape. That new Church will certainly put greater stress on the essentials of the priestly life and ministry, and it will provide a better context, challenge, and appreciation of the vowed dedication of religious. At the same time, though, the effective life and ministry of the Church in the years ahead will be rooted principally in laity.

In this book we will look at four aspects of the place of laity in the Church today.

In Chapter 1 we will consider the theological models of laity current in the Church today. In doing so, we will review the writings on laity from around the sixties—the preparatory years for Vatican II—and up to the present day. In these writings we will discover five trends or theological approaches to lay life. These theologies need to be clarified before serious dialogue can take place, since people often arrive at different answers to questions about laity because they are working out of different theologies.

In Chapter 2 we will look at developments and changes in attitudes and in Church structures that have occurred since the Council. We will identify strengths and weaknesses in the Church's post-conciliar approach to laity. Has the vision of the Council been effectively actualized in the Church over the last twenty years, or not? In answering, we will concentrate on three major areas of concern: ecclesial responsibility, spiritual life and growth, and mission and ministry.

Chapter 3 will present an understanding of the Church as family—an understanding that is suitable for a lay-centered Church. This understanding will imply a synthesis that is theologically powerful but still sufficiently part of the layperson's everyday life to be understood by all the baptized, not just by a theological elite. Moreover, the presentation of the Church as family is not abstract, as previous models have been, but rather challenges all laity to appreciate that their everyday experience, knowledge, and skills qualify them to be the family of the Church. So we will concentrate on the Church as family, seeing in this approach a model that satisfies many of these requirements.

Chapter 4 will review developments in historical and contemporary spirituality and will identify trends that are important for a present-day spirituality of all the baptized.

I offer these reflections as a service to all Christians. For all Catholic clergy and laity alike, they document trends of the present and recent past, give a historical background for some of the problems we currently face in the Church, and synthesize insights and theological positions of a very wide range of scholars and pastoral experts. For those who desire it, the documentation and bibliographical references given here are among the most detailed available in the area of theology of laity. However, I have kept these principally in endnotes so that the basic text can be read, understood, and appreciated by non-scholars in parishes throughout the nation. While giving the necessary theological foundation, I have at the same time focused throughout on issues that translate into practical, everyday concerns. In the next decade we must capitalize on the growing importance of the layperson, identify his or her rights, duties, ministry, and spirituality. All this must be done by laity with a sense of theological responsibility. Respecting a growing number of laypersons' commitment to this task, I have focused on the theological foundations.

Recent trends in lay development are not exclusive to the Roman Catholic Church, but are felt throughout all the traditions. Just as the Catholic Church has benefited from studies of other traditions, I am hopeful that these reflections will serve other Christian churches too. Ecclesial restructuring, priesthood of all the baptized, universal co-responsibility, a focus on family, and a general upgrading of the image of all the baptized are aspects of Christianity that all Christians share. The Catholic experience can be a major aid to other churches as theirs has been to the Catholic Church.

In the next ten to fifteen years, every baptized Christian will need to accept responsibility for his or her faith. Each one will need a reasoned, well-founded view of what it means to be a baptized person. I am hopeful that these pages will contribute to that vision.

1

Theologies of the Laity Since Vatican II: An Overview

Introduction

Future historians of theology and spiritual theology will undoubtedly look back on the twenty years following Vatican II as a great period in the development of a theological understanding of the role of the layperson, even though there is a clear decrease in attention given to the specific topic of laity. The enthusiasm of the immediate post-Council period, with its prolific publications on laity, soon waned and rapidly gave birth to discouragement at scholars' seeming lack of concern about laity. The feelings of the signers of the Chicago Declaration of Christian Concern are typical:

> Although the teaching of Vatican II on the ministry of the laity is forceful and represents one of the Council's most notable achievements, in recent years it seems to have all but vanished from the consciousness and agendas of many sectors within the Church.[1]

True, there has been a clearly identifiable decrease in publications on the specific topic of laity.[2] But the recent work of scriptural scholars, theologians, ecclesiologists, and historians, on the one hand, and the recent experience of the Church in spiritual movements, parish and community living, liberation theology and social justice involvement, ministries, and family living, on the other hand, are providing that substantial reflection and life experience that form the basis for an in-depth synthesis that these coming years will bring.

The years since the Council have been valuable regarding

the theology of the laity, both in the results produced and in the problems and confusion that have cried out for a theological solution. Strengths have been celebrated, and weaknesses have been identified.

In the years of the Council there was great interest in all aspects of lay apostolate, spirituality, theology, and ministry. People felt something new in the air. It was a period of change, newness, and hope. People spoke and wrote about lay collaboration and involvement; new roles for laity were opened up in parish life, education, ecumenism, and Church finance. Many articles in both scholarly and popular reviews during those years emphasized *the emerging role of the layperson* in the Church. The general euphoria was contagious, but the underlying theology was unfortunately not always clear.[3]

In the immediate post-Council years, new areas of work and apostolate were developed. Bishops throughout the world tried to provide apostolic openings for the laity, who were being challenged to be more aware of their baptismal responsibilities. This was the period of *opportunities*—suggested also in articles from all sides. Writings, at this time mainly in popular religious magazines, cited the need for continuing dialogue in order to maintain the strong relationship between the hierarchy and the laity with their newly fostered creative responsibility.

The years 1967 and 1968 were a time of continued opportunities and experiment. The interest aroused in previous years was now satisfied for many in the organization and development of spiritual movements. It was at this time that we saw an increased interest in the Cursillo, Focolare, Movement for a Better World, and similar movements. Unfortunately, scholarly writings at this time were few, and the torch of lay interest was carried mainly in religious newspapers and parish magazines. The main characteristic of these years was *national and international organization* of the laity. This was so both locally in the spiritual movements and internationally with such consolidation of lay efforts as was suggested in the Third World Congress on the Lay

Apostolate.

The next two years, 1969 and 1970, were years of *initial doubts and questioning* regarding the direction to take in lay spirituality. Some feared that emphasis on lay opportunities was not sufficiently complemented by the development of the lay-hierarchy relationship. This fear led some to abandon both their involvement in and their facilitating of lay ministry. Paul VI remained almost alone at this time in giving public support and directions for lay apostolate. Typical of his support were his encouraging addresses to the Commission for the Laity and other international lay organizations. However, the silence, the doubts, and the questioning of others were also valuable. Richard P. McBrien, at the beginning of an outstanding article, put into words the feeling of many:

> I should regard this essay a success if it becomes the last article written on the theology of the laity. Otherwise, I shall have contributed one more item to a body of literature which, as a systematic theologian, I can find little reason to justify. The topic itself betrays an understanding of the Church which is simply untenable; namely, that the non-ordained constitute a special segment of the Body of Christ whose vocation, dignity, and mission are somehow regarded as a limited aspect of the total vocation, dignity, and mission of the Church.[4]

McBrien's wish that his would be the last article on the theology of the laity was almost granted, and the following biennium was characterized by seemingly *decreased interest on a total ecclesial level.* Only such spiritual movements as Cursillo, the charismatic movement, and family groups kept lay involvement alive. In 1973 and 1974 some renewed interest was stimulated by the reprinting of works emphasizing *lay apostolate and world responsibility.*

However, it was the doubts and questioning of the previous five years that began to come to a head in 1975 and 1976. For the first time since the Council there was an increase in scholarly interest, but most scholarly discourse indicated a continued questioning and a *dissatisfaction and frustration* with the current explanations of the lay position in the Church.[5] In 1977 and 1978 this dissatisfaction led to serious thought about the *relationship of laity to hierarchy.* During this period we see the very positive move toward integrating lay theology into ecclesiology. Efforts were made to specify the role of laity in decision making in the Church and in ecclesial structures in general. The years 1979 and 1980 continued the trends of the previous two years. Some expressed *fears of lay role regression,*[6] but in many dioceses lay persons were integrated into the whole life of the Church. The trend in 1981 and 1982 was to concentrate on the *interrelationship in ministry* of hierarchy and laity. This emphasis was manifested also in increased publications on the topic. Further discussion, together with added lay experience in ministry, led in 1983 and 1984 to concentration on the difficult issue of *ministry and role clarification,* a topic whose importance was heightened by the promulgation in 1983 of the new Code of Canon Law. The Council was unable to arrive at a mature theological definition of the Christian layperson, and this is understandable.[7] Rather than presenting a finished theological evaluation of the layperson's life and ministry, the Council's new insights in ecclesiology became the starting point for a new understanding of the layperson. The years since Vatican II, however, have seen major swings in theological reflection on laity, and wonderful developments in the life-styles of many laypersons. As we look around the Church today, we see several underlying theologies of laity, and these are what I will now consider. In each case I will present the theological position, with detailed reference to the authors and movements that support it, and then offer some evaluative comments.

Theology of Instrumental Ministry

Historical and contemporary manifestations
On 30 March 1930, Pius XI announced the official organi-

zation of "Catholic Action" for Italy. Under his personal direction and support, Catholic Action spread extensively. The underlying theology of laity identifiable in a Catholic Action-type emphasis was highly respected right up to the papal initiatives of Pius XII and John XXIII and is still very much alive today.[8] Basically, Catholic Action was the international organizing and consolidating of corporate and ecclesiastically recognized apostolic initiatives undertaken by laity throughout the world. It did not claim or desire any monopoly on lay involvement, and individuals and groups were free to be spontaneously apostolic even if they were not part of Catholic Action. However, there was a certain quality associated with having one's work officially recognized by the Church. A lay group which had been officially recognized and mandated was considered to be participating in the apostolate of the Church's hierarchy and was thus seen as an arm of the hierarchy.

The assumption of this model is that it is to the hierarchy and only to the hierarchy that Jesus entrusted the Church's mission.

In recent years, theology has often emphasized this institutionalized approach to lay activity, seeing that activity as based on an ecclesiastical mandate. In the first major Congress of Laity in his pontificate, Paul VI stated the theological position clearly:

> Indeed no one can take it amiss that the normal instrumental cause of divine designs is the Hierarchy, or that, in the Church, efficacy is proportional to one's adherence to those whom Christ "has made guardians to feed the Church of the Lord." Anyone who attempts to act without the Hierarchy, or against it . . . could be compared to a branch which atrophies because it is no longer connected with the stem which provided its sap.[9]

In this theological position, laity were free to be spontaneously involved in apostolic activity. But, given the position of the hierarchy, it was clearly better to be organized under their direction and in some way to be an arm of the hierarchy extended to the world.

In 1971 Rome set up the Council of Laity to deal with international lay organizations. This Council explicitly allowed the laity to form spontaneous groups, but these were not to be considered official parts of the Church's apostolate, a position reaffirmed by the new Code of Canon law.[10]

The Detroit "Call to Action," held in 1976, was specifically set up by the hierarchy to aid them in *their* apostolic work, and the bishops' meeting in Chicago in November 1977 reiterated the purpose of the Detroit meeting, its restrictions, and its value for the *hierarchy's* apostolate. The different theologies of laity held by conveners and participants were almost certainly the basic cause of many of the Detroit meeting's problems.[11]

In January of 1977, Pope Paul set up the Pontifical Council of the Laity. This had been called the Council of the Laity from 1971 to 1976, but by being drawn into the higher levels of Roman administration it became a more intimate and important part of the hierarchy's apostolic work. Unfortunately, prevailing Church law excluded laity from that level of involvement in the Church's mission, and clerics had to be appointed to those positions previously occupied by the laity.[12]

In April of 1978, the National Conference of Catholic Bishops' Committee on the Laity met and clearly indicated yet again in several ways its factual preference for a theology of the laity that presents the laity as auxiliaries and supporters of the bishops in their work.[13]

In addition to these special events of recent years, many dioceses have set up lay ministries. Frequently, there are special ceremonies in which the bishop or pastor, at times with the imposition of hands, mandates the laity for specific ministries. This approach is a further manifestation of the theological conviction that authorization from the hierarchy is necessary for one to participate officially in the Church's mission.

Notable strengths of this position

There are notable strengths to this theology of instrumental ministry. The Church is the sacrament of unity, and this theology highlights the unity of the whole people in Jesus Christ, whose present-day "apostolate in the full sense of the mandate-mission belongs to the hierarchy."[14] According to Paul VI, this approach is also a clear affirmation of Catholic identity and permanently facilitates reflection, meditation, and constant integration of lay ministry with the gospel and the magisterium of the Church.[15] The dynamic interrelationship between hierarchy and laity brings the liturgical, sacramental, transformational, and sanctifying essence of the Church to the world. In this view, "the Christian laity is the point where the leaven of the Gospel is thrust full into the meal of the world and meets its historical reality."[16] For those laity who live this instrumental ministry, the different roles of the hierarchy and laity, the recognition of power and authority, and the mutual service and humility this ministry demands are part of the very asceticism of being Church. Two decades ago Gérard Philips expressed this well:

> If a dissident Christian were reading this . . . he would certainly be struck by the hierarchical tone that surrounds the description of the laity. If a Protestant, he would wonder whether in the presence of such extensive authority there remains any liberty for the harassed and stifled Catholic. . . . He sees himself faced with a choice whereas the Catholic embraces the two.[17]

Recent questioning of this position

This model is extensively supported and lived. However, the theology of this approach has been seriously questioned in recent years. Many theologians have voiced concern over identifying the mission of the Church with the function of the hierarchy. They point out that this assumption can easily lead to clericalization and power positions within the hierarchy and to a lack of initiative and personal responsibility among the laity.[18]

As early as 1968, Edward Schillebeeckx rejected "in principle any tendency to view the apostolate of the laity . . . only as a kind of participation in the hierarchical apostolate." McBrien in 1969 and 1973 stated that "it is difficult to reconcile that particular notion of the lay apostolate with the clear teachings of Vatican II . . .," and he goes on to add:

> There is no mention here [in Vatican II] that the laity shares in the mission of the Church only to the extent that the hierarchy allows. The mission comes from Christ through the sacraments, and not through the leadership personnel of the Church.[19]

Even Yves Congar, who had seemingly given so much support to the instrumental concept, refers in his later writings to its insufficiency.[20] Christian Duquoc, along with others, appeals for a new ecclesiology and a new understanding of mission, and he insightfully adds that the theology of instrumental ministry would threaten the laity's unique contribution to the Church's life.[21]

The instrumental ministry approach has been an excellent contribution to the life of the Church and has highlighted the profound values in ministerial priesthood and hierarchy. Moreover, given the previously poor education of laity, it was the best approach for its time. But the developments in ecclesiology initiated by Vatican II and the increased education of laity now seem to demand a different approach.

Theology of Ecclesial Presence to the World

Theological foundations for this model

As Schillebeeckx has pointed out, "History shows that the role of the laity was not really and fully recognized until man himself discovered the value of the world."[22] The great preconciliar studies of Gustave Thils and M. D. Chenu opened up the road to a new approach to the theology of laity, and other excellent complementary studies highlighted the intrinsic value of the world. The erroneous theological views of matter and world, which had often appeared throughout Christian history, had been a major block to the development of a theology of laity. The "world" was often seen as the work of the Evil One or, at best, as an "occasion" for doing good when "intention" somehow gave a religious value to work that in itself had no eternal significance.[23] The studies just referred to, however, see the world as intrinsically good, as the theatre of ecclesial development; work well done is no longer a means but an end in itself (though a secondary one). Moreover, the Council explicitly identifies the Church as a sacrament of the world, in the world, to serve the world (*Church* 9; *Church Today* 45). This reevaluation of the world has had immense importance in the development of a theology of laity, for it is the laity who are seen as the bridge between Church and world, the Church's presence to the world.[24]

This theological evaluation of the life and role of the layperson has received substantial consideration from theologians. The major pre-conciliar works of Congar, Karl Rahner, and Schillebeeckx became the focal points for the theological evaluation of the specifics of lay life.[25] Their insights were incorporated into Vatican II's explanations, and most post-conciliar studies either developed their thought or reacted against it. Most books in the hands of a theology-reading laity today support in large measure the conviction that the laity are the Church's presence to the world.[26]

The basic premise of this theological understanding is the conviction that earthly and temporal realities have a value and a goodness of their own, and that the Church is sent precisely into this earthly, temporal sphere.[27] This view was prepared for by the process of secularization, was aided by the theologies of work and the studies on eschatology, and was confirmed by the Council's definition of the Church as sacrament of the world. Vatican II formulated this conclusion:

[God] intends in Christ to appropriate the whole universe into a new creation, initially here on earth, fully on the last day. (L 5:1)

The layperson is the one through whom God achieves this goal.

In the attainment of all these goals, laymen have the greatest importance and deserve special attention. These are those Christians who have been incorporated into Christ by baptism and who live in the world.[28]

The layperson, who belongs neither to the hierarchy nor to a community of religious, is here viewed as an active member of the ecclesial people of God and is called to incarnate himself or herself as sacrament of the world in the specific circumstances of secular life. Through the layperson's work, individuals and informal groups, as well as groups and organizations not directly related to the Church's control, are placed in contact with the Church's saving mission. According to the authors referred to, the layperson is not the extension of the hierarchy but has a specific and exclusively proper mission in secular situation.[29]

... the layman is the Christian whose Christian situation and responsibilities are determined from below, by his insertion in the life of the world, though he has to live that situation and those responsibilities as a Christian.
... the layman also sanctifies himself precisely in this secular involvement, and his apostolic activity is carried on first and foremost through secular involvement.[30]

According to this theology, what are the specifics of the layperson's ministry? In this view, the world is not only sinful and against God, as previous theologians had stressed, but is also the object of God's love, and laypersons are to be "the visible presence in history, space and time of the redemptive grace of God in Jesus Christ."[31] In their daily tasks and in life-situations of marriage, society, and public life, which are laypersons' normal way of self-realization and perfection, they are to be incarnated as a spiritual presence; they are to create an atmosphere conducive to a God-directed life, extend Christ's love and peace to the world order, oppose sinful situations, and transform our world into resurrection hope.[32]

In this theology we are dealing with an area where the Church ministers through influence, not through hierarchical power. Laypersons are committed to the secular; they are really in the world; they know and love it; they identify with its values, and through the grace of the sacrament of baptism and aided by personal charisms they influence, inspire, and direct the world. They strive to make world values (culture, education, and peace) accessible to all; they challenge society to grow, and they are heralds of faith and hope.[33]

Positive aspects of this theology

This theology of laity gives renewed importance to the world, to temporal realities, and to the layperson's work here. This rids Christian spirituality of exaggerated spiritualism and of an unreasonable departmentalization of life, and it corrects the frequent erroneous interpretation of "flight from the world."[34] It strongly confirms a theology of work for laypersons—work in which they are constructively involved in something intrinsically valuable and in the exercise of which they themselves grow.[35] Christian laity who put their convictions into practice each day in the changing circumstances of their lives highlight the ever-newness of the Christ-message and its permanent relevance to the ever-changing lay situations.

Furthermore, the very fact that we can discuss a specific and proper lay role eliminates the ecclesiologically unacceptable aspects of the previous theology of instrumental ministry. The theology of ecclesial presence to the world instead strengthens faith in the mystery and divine values of our world and thereby integrates into Western theology some of the values of the Greek Fathers.[36] In particular, this openness to the world and this appreciation of the specific contributions of all the baptized makes us Christian in attitudes as well as in name.

Some problems in this position

Widespread and important though this position is, it also has some problems. The original theological positions of Rahner and Schillebeeckx have been severely criticized. Unfortunately, Philips and Congar, who were among the critics, are themselves basically exponents of this theology.[37] These theologians, wanting to define the layperson as a believer "in the world," seemed rather to portray the layperson as "worldly" and uninterested in the things of God. Although these theologians continued to hold ground until the seventies, their basic ideas are founded on pre-conciliar ecclesiology. The laity are not a bridge between Church and world; the laity *are* Church. Nor is the superficial distinction between "priest/sacred" and "lay/temporal" acceptable, since the laity are not confined to the temporal sphere of life but are also called to be actively involved in the liturgy. Moreover, neither are priests and religious confined exclusively to the sacred, since their vowed lives challenge the misuse of secular values of wealth, sexual love, and power. Finally, prayer and contemplation for the layperson have been poorly developed in this theology of ecclesial presence to the world.

Theologians associated with this position started by proclaiming the need for a theology of earthly realities, and there was truth and insight in this. But more was needed. A new ecclesiology needed to be developed: an ecclesiology that reemphasized the importance of the contributions of every baptized Christian.

Theology of World Transformation

Description of this approach

The theology of the laity that emphasized world transformation is germinally present in the Council documents and is implicit in the theology of ecclesial presence to the world. However, the theologians referred to in the previous section are not the ones responsible for the theology of world transformation, despite their initial insights. The theology of world transformation was arrived at by those who reflected on the tenets of ecclesial presence and by those lay people who, once committed to the life-style implied in that model, realized that one is not truly present to the world without attempting to transform the world. In the theological position of world transformation, then, the layperson is not only *in* the world but *for* the world. But this world does not correspond to the way God willed it; rather, it is a world in process of becoming in Christ what it is capable of being. It is not enough to view the world statically; it must be approached with an awareness that we are called to change it—to redeem it to the glory of God. This approach teaches that asceticism of the laity is "an inner element of faith's responsibility for the world."[38]

Theological reflection since the Council years has offered excellent contributions in methodology, scripture studies, Christology, and spirituality—all of which have aided the clear formulation of a theology of world transformation.[39]

This position emphasizes that the world is not only the context of our redemption but itself needs to be redeemed. The world, with all its immense possibilities, has been entrusted to the responsibility of human beings who now participate in redeeming it. World development is intimately connected with the final subjection of all to Christ. The consensus of contributions to this position is that the incarnational approach must in the last analysis center on Christ's ongoing redemption of the world. The role and mission of the layperson in this theological position becomes clear and well defined.

> God's plan for the world is that men should work together to restore the temporal sphere of things and to develop it unceasingly.
>
> For the Lord wishes to spread His kingdom by

means of the laity also, a kingdom of truth and life, a kingdom of holiness and grace, a kingdom of justice, love, and peace. In this kingdom, creation itself will be delivered out of its slavery to corruption and into the freedom of the glory of the sons of God.[40]

In this theology, laypersons are agents in the consecration of the universe to God.[41] They are committed to the world, use it with detachment, heal it of sin, animate it with Christ's spirit, transform it into what it is capable of being, dominate it, and consecrate the world to God in Christ.[42]

Those who are aware of the intrinsic goodness of the world and who are dedicated to developing and transforming that world tend to be aware not only of individual sin, but also of social, structuralized sin. Consequently, the theology of world transformation is best seen today in the lay groups dedicated to social justice issues, in the worldwide movements of political and liberation theology, and in the writings that these produce.

Strengths and value of this position

In this theology of world transformation, the laity serve the world and prophetically challenge it in areas of work, family values, politics, business, trade unions, government, stock exchanges, employment, and so on. In other words, Christian commitment is seen in this theology as dominating social evolution and, through creativity in providing alternatives in social life, as prophetically giving the world a path to follow.[43] "Is it not the laity who are called, by reason of their vocation in the Church, to make their contribution in the political and economic dimensions, and to be effectively present in the safeguarding and advancement of human rights?"[44]

This particular theology of laity, reflecting a profound reading of scripture, values the secular world as it is, and also values positively whatever contributes to its development. It highlights the nobility and eternal significance of human action and involvement in human progress. It encourages the development of one's own personality as a part of spiritual growth. It gives faith-incentives for being energetically involved in the development of civic, national, and international life.[45] In so doing, it removes both that sense of indifference to this world and the duality of Church/world so frequently seen in Christians, for it brings the light of faith to bear on human values and expresses a renewed appreciation of the historical and eschatological centrality of Christ, who is the key to history and world development. Consequently, the layperson's dedication to world transformation is finally concretized in Christ in the Church. "The cosmos can come to fulfillment in Christ through the Church just as conversely the Church will only attain its true pleroma when the material and non-material cosmos has been brought into its 'Catholic,' totally comprehensive unity." This is done in the Eucharist, which is both the experience of world transformation and the pledge of future glory for the world.[46]

Integrating world values as it does with lay spiritual growth through human progress, commitment to remove injustice, and ecclesial and eucharistic life, this theology of laity is very strong and satisfying. John Paul II indicated in his Puebla address that this lay commitment to transform the world could not easily be taken over by others.[47] It is a specific of lay life.

Some shortcomings of this approach

A basic problem in this theology of laity is that it demands a radical conversion in the way one understands the essential contribution of earthly life to salvation. Many people find it difficult even to admit the need for such conversion, for "that the earthly and heavenly city penetrate each other is a fact accessible to faith alone" (CT 40:4; also C 48:3).

There are some other problems with this theology of world transformation. The laity's life and mission is more than world transformation. Laypersons immersed in this approach to life find it difficult to unite social transformation with prayer and liturgy. Religious movements frequently end up emphasizing sociological adaptation, and their members cease to lead a faith life. With involvement in world transformation and immediate life problems comes the risk of forgetting such basic and perennial aspects of Christian life as trust, abandonment to Providence, faith in Christ as eschatological healer, and acceptance of the mystery of suffering.[48] Moreover, so much spirituality has presented a picture diametrically opposed to this theology that it will take time to appreciate the essential link between faith and world development. In the meantime, adherents of this theology need to keep clearly in mind the distinction between our work and God's, so as to avoid ending in a new Pelagianism that in effect believes that world transformation is possible without God's grace.[49]

Theology of Laity and Ecclesial Restructuring

Trends calling for ecclesial restructuring

We have seen that the first great initiative in lay theology was made by Yves Congar. Twenty years after publication of his momentous *Lay People in the Church*, Congar reviewed his own journey of practically a quarter of a century through the area of lay theology. In this fine synthesis he presented his conviction that the developing theology of laity is now leading to ecclesial restructuring, and he indicated four reasons for this trend. First, he acknowledges that the study of the New Testament and of early Church history shows that some of our understandings of ecclesial structure are over-simplified, local, and relative. Second, he believes that Vatican II gave us a new direction in theology that includes valuing Christian experience over structure, an emphasis on ministries seen functionally, and a decentralization to the collegial at all levels. Third, he states that the ecumenical dialogue has challenged him and the Church as a whole to review the role of the layperson in Church decision making and structures. Fourth, he says that many scholars are questioning the relationship of authority to the Christian community; and this, he feels, is a question that theologians must seriously address.[50]

Several theological insights of recent decades led to this new understanding of the lay role. First was the move from an institutional to a community understanding of Church as seen in the Vatican II's Dogmatic Constitution on the *Church*. That document's emphasis on such terms as *mystery* and *People of God* before *hierarchy* was intended to show the conviction that hierarchy was a secondary structuring of the People of God; the Church is a community before it is a hierarchical institution.

Together with this new understanding of Church as community goes the Council's teaching on collegiality. While in its strict form this term refers only to bishops, it is nevertheless being interpreted and applied at all levels. The organizational model is now collegial rather than monarchical.[51]

Another contribution to this theology of laity and ecclesial restructuring is the broader understanding of mission as a function of the total Church rather than as a function of the hierarchy. Mission is seen here as resulting from baptism, confirmation, and personal charisms.[52]

The lives of many lay people today are based on the presupposition that the Church is really a community, collegially governed, with a mission resulting from baptism. Serious efforts are being made by clergy and laity alike to clarify the role of the layperson in the local Church structures.[53] According to Karl Rahner, these efforts are theologically sound and not in vain. When describing the shape of the Church to come, he speaks of a declericalized Church, a Church concerned with serving, a Church "from the roots," and a democratized Church.[54]

Such a Church will demand specific contributions from laity. Richard P. McBrien suggests that laity can effectively do their part in the following ways:

> . . . principally through the creation and effective operation of parish councils, diocesan pastoral councils, national pastoral councils, and through lay

participation on various policy making boards such as those supervising admissions to seminaries. Laity should also have some meaningful voice in the selection of their bishops and pastors, and in the ongoing evaluation of their pastoral performance.[55]

Other theologians are presenting participation in Church institutions as a sacramental and baptismal right, and they specify the implications of this.[56] Still others have pointed out specific areas of lay life and responsibility that result from this theological position, whether it be the task of honest evaluation of ecclesiastical policy or education or ministry or strictly theological input.[57]

In addition to the formulations of theologians, there are other signs of this theological view of the laity's position, with its resulting call for ecclesial restructuring. The first is the development of "basic ecclesial communities." These developed after 1968, first in France and later in Latin America, initially as a reaction to overstructure. In general, they have the characteristics and hopes I have indicated above. These free, spontaneous, informal groups generally stress faith development, political involvement, and often, liturgical experimentation. Many bishops have supported and deliberately initiated the organization of basic ecclesial communities. When guided away from certain excesses, the groups have often proved to be strengtheners of local Church life. Their inner organization is simple and often intervocational, and it gives specific roles and decision-making authority to lay participants.

A second emphasis today that seems at least an implicit statement of ecclesial restructuring is the strong and frequent formulation of the doctrine of the common priesthood. In this view, "the prime priestly reality is the priesthood of the faithful" that is received in baptism. Lay life and ministry develop from this common priesthood without need of further mandate or authorization.[58] Consequently, a regrouping of laity according to areas of professional involvement or interest is now often seen as an exercise of common priesthood. Ministerial priesthood is then understood as service to this common priesthood, and its functions are reiterated accordingly.

A third emphasis that implies ecclesial restructuring is the development of some areas of lay ministry. Lay ministries are sometimes understood to be extended instrumental ministry. While this is true in some instances, as I have already mentioned, in other cases we are dealing with such ministries as religious education, catechetical instruction, sacramental preparation, some liturgical ministries, evangelization, and proclamation of the Word. The important point is that many of these ministries develop from real needs, already exist, and are effective without any formal acceptance by the hierarchy, even though this acceptance may be given later.[59] Then again there are many intervocational team ministries today where authority and hierarchy are lived differently from the major model of the institutional Church. Other powerful ministries in family life, politics, social involvement, health, and education have led to a different way of understanding the essentials of Church. Many lay ministries manifest or lead to a different view of laity in the Church.[60]

Positive values of this position

This particular theological emphasis that I have grouped under ecclesial restructuring has some notable strengths. It portrays the essential equality of the People of God. It respects the layperson and values the constitutive community of the Church. It highlights co-responsibility and intervocational ministry as resulting from baptism. It expands the notion of ministry for lay people and fosters specialization in ministry. In addition, it focuses attention on the essentials of the minister-priest's role. As a result, many areas of work and ministry previously dealt with by the priest are now handled by laity, which leaves the priestly minister freer for sacramental ministry and spiritual direction.

Problems: A theology in transition

However, this theological position has some problems,[61]

not the least of which is that it is restricted to laity who are fully involved in ministry, and that it seems to imply a devaluing of the unique role of the ordinary Christian who does nothing "extra." The turning in on problems of Church structure has a touch of narcissism about it and sometimes just results in reversed roles wherein laity take on dominant authority in newly created structures. The needed emphasis on Church-related issues has often resulted in neglect of some of those areas admirably dealt with by theologies discussed previously, e.g., world involvement.

This approach seems to be in transition at the moment, but if communication barriers can come down, and if honest evaluation can take place, then this theological position will pay high dividends in lay life and in priestly life and ministry, too.

Theology of Self-Discovery for Laity

Situational involvement

At the end of his book on the role of the laity, Gérard Philips acknowledged that many theological problems lay ahead, but he added, "Life works out a problem when the theologians can't." Certainly there are problems, and the theology of laity remains in a stage of development and speculation, not least because the Vatican Council "provides such a forceful portrait that many decades will pass before all of its possibilities will become a learning shared by all Christians."[62]

We may not yet have a mature theology of the laity or, rather, a final ecclesiology that makes a theology of laity unnecessary. But in the meantime the laity are discovering ever-new challenges in their life and mission.

Many laypeople now see that they need to be very open and flexible and ready to reincarnate the basic Christian challenges in our ever-changing society. We have a sort of "situational lay spirituality."

In the more extensive life experiences of family, politics,

social developments, justice issues, and so on, people throughout the world are now paying more attention to the contributions of the lay Christian. It is the layperson who must be a prophetical challenge to modern values. Moreover, many laypeople are doing precisely this in small groups in many cities, sometimes with priests or religious, sometimes on their own. Study groups and faith-supportive groups are increasing in number. Their purpose is growth in faith, and their mission is to challenge one or other of society's pseudo-values.[63] In a world that emphasizes consumerism, some laity live simple lives; in a world seemingly dedicated to the rat race, others opt for quality of life; when society stresses sexual freedom, some lay Christians stand for the dignity of the human person.

In some geographical areas suffering from a drastic loss of priests, new ministries are opening to the laity, and laity are coping or creatively developing.[64] Some few Christians are responding to the signs of the times by answering a call to simplicity and poverty and liberation. In some ways, the Detroit "Call to Action" was really a "call to what we think we could be."

Many of the religious organizations and spiritual movements of recent years are situational: They creatively respond to a specific need.[65] Some such organizations and movements are internationally organized, but more frequently they are looser function-based groups locally organized by laity.

In all of the above situations, some laity are responding when a need is seen; when the need ends, so does the group's mission. However, these experiences of laypeople are important for the Church and for any further theology of laity.

Theology is reflection, a critical attitude. First comes the commitment to charity, to service. Theology comes "later." It is second. The Church's pastoral action is not arrived at as a conclusion from theological premises. Theology does not lead to pastoral activity, but is rather a reflection on it. Theology should find the spirit present in it, inspiring the actions of the Christian community.[66]

In other words, theology critically reflects on the daily situations of laity. Their Christian living becomes a source for theological reflection. Present experiences of laity are closely interrelated with theology. New creative situational involvement and lay dedication will give rise in future decades to new directions in theological reflection.

Contributing to this process will also be the ecclesial experience of intervocational groups, movements, and ministries, wherein priests, religious, and laypeople work together. What does a prolonged ecclesial experience of this sort say about lay life and its contribution to Church?

The examples I have given do not "fit in" to previous theologies. They are ad hoc responses and new approaches to life experiences. They are not only areas of ministry; they are life-styles, too. In time, theology will take account of them.[67] These strivings should be grouped together under a theology of self-discovery for laity.

Positive strivings in faith and love

Positively, these strivings toward self-discovery are manifestations of faith and charity. They highlight a search and a desire in many to lead committed lives. Continual self-discovery heralds growth. Moreover, in their search many Christians are experiencing God in a way not known before, and we can only rejoice in this. The fact that most discovery situations are group commitments is contributing immensely to the community dimension of the Church. This heuristic or exploratory approach is encouraging and hope-filled.

Shortcoming:
A decreased sense of belonging to a structured Church

Unfortunately, there is sometimes a decrease in a sense of belonging to the Church, which can end up as a psychological opting out of structured Church. Not all creative involvement is theologically possible, and if religious education is weak, the end result is neglect of fundamentals of faith.[68]

Conclusion:
A Theology of Laity as Integrally Church

Throughout this chapter I have spoken of theologies of *the laity*. Nevertheless, I am convinced that the term *laity* is now theologically dead. Originally it meant "the people of God," "the ecclesial people." The word now has many theologically erroneous positions attached to its normal everyday meaning and use, and so it seems to concretize within itself the history of our mistakes.

It emphasizes the distinction between sacred and profane as if we were dealing with two histories rather than, as faith tells us, "a single human progress, irreversibly exalted by Christ, the Lord of history . . . [whose] redemptive work embraces every dimension of human existence."[69] When *laity* is used to designate those who passively receive from the Church, and *hierarchy* designates those who are active mediators with God, it often creates an image of a God who is only indirectly accessible.

The very question of the role of the layperson in the Church today is often approached with the assumption that the Church is basically clerical.[70] On the level of daily living, the laity frequently see themselves as on the receiving end of the intra-Church system at a time when, as Schillebeeckx pointed out in 1969, "the twentieth century is experiencing the bankruptcy of all systems, including Christianity as a monological system."[71] Moreover, we search to identify the position of the layperson in the Church "as if this were a real point of discussion. Biblically and theologically, the problem should be posed exactly the other way around: What is the place of ministry in the ecclesial people of God?"[72] Approaches to the layperson's position and spirituality often convey the "teaching" that bodily activity, senses, feelings, worldly realities, and activity in the world are of secondary value for the kingdom.

The clergy/laity distinction has set up many false problems for the Church, and will go on doing so as long as
it is retained, since it represents a principle alien to the
nature of the Church as a society. Talk of a "distinctively
clerical" or a "distinctively lay" point of view is
nonsense.[73]

Laypersons do not *belong to* the Church, nor do they *have
a role in* the Church. Rather, through baptism they *are*
Church, and, in union with Christ, their mission is the
mission of the Church itself.[74] There is no particular vocation for laity in the Church, no need of a quest for lay
identity. Being Church in its fullness is the spirituality for
laity. This was one of Congar's insights in his initial discussion of the theology of laity: At bottom there can be only one
sound and sufficient theology of laity, and that is a "total
ecclesiology."[75]

Through the sacraments of initiation a person becomes
Church and is theologically challenged to live as integrally
Church. When I speak of laity as integrally Church, I mean
that they live out the full responsibility of their baptism and
confirmation. The Christian personality is essentially ecclesial. Fortunately, there is no instant Church, and the various
difficulties of continually growing into being Church are
precisely what constitute the asceticism of the baptized, for
the Church is a sacrament of unity. In this context, union,
dialogue, obedience, challenge, revision, criticism, and so
on, are not mutually exclusive. This Christian life must be
integrally Church, and to be Church means to live as a
community in the world for the service of the world. The
baptized person, therefore, is not only a member of the
Church who lives in the heart of the world, but is also a
member of the world community living at the heart of the
Church.[76]

Baptism challenges all to be and to live as community of
faith based on the Word and on the freedom and love that
Christ has brought. We are called to one and the same life.

Instead of looking for a theology *of* the laity, we need a theology *for* laity. The task is not to specify the lay mission, but to be educated to awareness of who we are in baptism. The way of approaching Church life and the way of approaching world life are formally different for varied vocations.[77] But this is not the emphasis needed today, except for the spirituality of priest and religious. What the baptized Christian needs is to become aware of being integrally Church.

As we look ahead, it is crucial that in all future efforts and developments, laity and hierarchy work together and discover together what they can be. In a period of increased lay responsibility, the hierarchy must not sacrifice what in faith we know they must be. All mediational roles must be preserved. Laity, responding to a baptismal commitment, must respond "as Church," with no trace of the individualism that has unfortunately characterized some and led to conflict between laity and the local diocesan administration. Individualistic responses "outside of Church," which generally involve a psychological opting out of Church as institution, are neither Catholic nor Christian. Laity must live out their responsibility with an awareness of what it means to be Church, appreciative of other ministries within this community. In the decades ahead, the mission of laity and the mission of hierarchy will grow interdependently. If we stress only one, our ecclesiology will be weak, but if we can develop both together we can anticipate a very positive future.

2

Laity in the Church Today
An Assessment of Attitudes and Structures

Introduction

In the 1960s the Vatican Council participants approved and published the documents on the *Church*, on the *Church in the Modern World*, and on the *Laity*. These three documents have had an enormous impact on our understanding of the role of the layperson today. They have been quoted more than any other ecclesiastical documents of recent times and have challenged all members of the Church to a new way of seeing themselves and to a new awareness of what it means to be Church.

Those intense and challenging Council discussions called for a new direction in ecclesiology and ministry, and they implied a movement of laity upward in ecclesial dignity and outward in responsible service.[1] But what have been the real results? When we confront the conciliar call with the lived reality of today, do we see an adequate and healthy embodiment of those teachings in the areas of ecclesial responsibility, spiritual life and growth, mission, and ministry? In the post-Council years of accelerated social and ecclesial change, are the expressions of our faith compatible with the Spirit-guided insights of Vatican II?

Many tensions have developed. Perhaps the most obvious tension between the faith of the Christian and the Council's challenge to examine the layperson's role has occurred in the area of attitudes. Some clergy have supposedly been willing to involve the laity, but fear has driven them to choose a "pastoral prudence" that has meant violating the baptismal rights of laypeople, who are also called to ministry in their Church.

Furthermore, a deep-seated attitude equating laity with the purely secular has often limited lay ministry to areas of management and finance, with the result that both laity and clergy are frustrated at the lack of spiritual and religious content in such ministry.

But perhaps the greatest struggle resulting from examining the layperson's role in the Church has centered on so-called "sacred traditions," such as those that claim exclusively hierarchical rights to teach, preach, or govern. Since these traditions can rarely be traced back to the early Church, they can no longer be preserved at the cost of such essential elements of Christianity as baptismal equality, universal call to ministry, and participation in the development of Church life.

At the same time, there have been many changes in the Church since Vatican II. Some of these changes are the result of profound societal developments that have their counterparts in Church life. The new approaches we have seen in civil society to social justice, sexuality, technology, women's issues, and institutional oppression have also been seen in the Church.

In this chapter, however, we are not primarily concerned with these changes that the Church has experienced and shared with all societies. Rather, we are principally concerned with discussing the Church's contributions in post-Council years to a clearer understanding and development of the place of laity within the Church. In our survey we will review the Church's sense of the laity's ecclesial responsibility, evaluate lay spiritual life and growth, and examine the Church's acceptance of lay mission and ministry. Various approaches to the laity's role, life, and ministry are identifiable in the Church today. On the one hand, these different approaches have resulted in practical pastoral problems that need resolution and redirection. On the other hand, these different approaches also have theological implications that we need to consider.

Since the way the Church lives out its message and

teaching is part of its very fidelity or infidelity to the Lord, and since the Church's future is generally determined by the way it responds in the present, this issue of the integration of the laity into the Church lets us glimpse both the Church's fidelity to the hopes of Vatican II and also the likely future directions of a pilgrim people.

Laity and Their Ecclesial Responsibility

The teachings of the Second Vatican Council,[2] together with a series of outstanding post-conciliar documents,[3] have given us a superb starting point for a rich and developing image of the layperson. The laity's awareness of their newly described image, together with their commitment to accept the implied challenges, is one of the characteristics of the Church of our times. It is an irreversible phenomenon of the Church in renewal.[4] Grass-roots renewal efforts have also stressed the Spirit's gifts to each one and have called for a committed use of all charisms for the Church. Renewal—particularly in parish life, liturgy, spiritual movements and groups, and local ecclesial ministries—has fostered lay involvement and has implied a new understanding of the lay role in the Church. In short, in these post-Vatican II years we have shared in a great ecclesial rediscovery of our heritage, particularly in ministry, from the early Church.

Lay involvement in this rediscovery has not been a mainstream renewal. This involvement has either been achieved through the spiritual movements outside of regular ecclesiastical structures or has been restricted to a committed minority within local Church structures. The position of the vast majority of laity has remained unchanged, and they want it that way. Why? Because some simply want to be left alone; they do not want to assume any active leadership role. Many others have been alienated by post-conciliar, internal Church crises such as those dealing with Church structures, where conflict and polarization regarding the use of authority have arisen at all levels, from papal government to local parish councils. Others have been alienated by crises centering around Church persons, such as the crises in the roles of priests and religious. Still others have been alienated by crises centering around doctrine, where different interpretations either provoke division or at least maintain it. For still others, a general lack of education and a lack of understanding of the need for change has led to a sense of insecurity that has entrenched them in pre-Vatican II outward forms of Church life. We see this in groups that have already returned to pre-Vatican II liturgies or forms of religious life or clerical dominance or local diocesan structures.

Many laity today never actually say what they think of current efforts to integrate the laity into Church life; they simply protest with their feet and leave the Church. Others remain within established structures but find nourishment for their spiritual life elsewhere in spontaneous religious sharing of prayer groups and faith-sharing groups. Hans Küng warned against this spontaneous religious sharing soon after the Council: "Outbreaks of enthusiasm are always signs of a crisis, usually a crisis of scriptural doctrine or of Church order."[5] Other laity appear to remain in the Church but actually live differently and think differently from what is presumed: They live in a hierarchical Church but would prefer a democratic style of government; they do not discuss clerical celibacy but see little value or purpose in it; they attend Sunday service but find little spiritual sustenance there; they are totally uninterested and uninfluenced by many ecclesiastical decisions. The authors of a recent study of laity in suburban parishes concluded that the laity in their daily lives and convictions neither accept nor live any of the current understandings of the Church proposed by clerics and theologians. In fact, the laity's priorities and convictions implied that they see the Church differently from the way the hierarchy and clerics do.[6] The two groups live in the Church with understandings that are either parallel or diverging, but certainly these understandings do not and most likely will not meet.

These basically psychological or sociological lay attitudes

are very significant and must be taken into account by the universal Church.

For those clergy and laity, however, who have taken seriously the new understanding of the lay role, what has been done in the area of ecclesial responsibility? In the following sections I would like to review developments in structures and authority, in the recognition of rights and duties, and in fostering collaboration in a common vision.

Structures and authority

The relationship between the laity and the structures and authority of the Church has been a central issue of debate ever since the Council. The Council itself spoke about profound changes that have occurred in institutions as a result of cultural and social change (CT 73:1), but we have not yet witnessed profound changes in the institutional Church. It is unquestionable that many leaders in the institutional Church have responded to the gospel call (see Mk. 10:43-45) and now live the awareness that all Church power is for ecclesial service. However, this realization is difficult to live out when the major structures of the Church are entirely clerical and at times oppress the laity.

The total absence of laity from leadership roles, even from those Church organizations specifically for laity, is an extremely unhealthy dimension of the Church. Power in the Church is linked to office, not to competence, and even non-sacramental jurisdiction is granted only to the cleric. It seems unlikely that this will change, since Canon Law is written principally by clerics to govern a clerical Church. In the meantime, as key Church leaders grow older, they tend to become more conservative.

At one time the cardinals were the *lay* advisers to the bishop of Rome, but not many years ago Paul VI insisted that all cardinals be bishops. The Pontifical Council for the Laity is governed by clerics, and the 1980 Synod on the family allowed only a few carefully screened lay *observers* to attend, while the Church's teaching on family and sexuality was debated exclusively by celibate clerics.

As far as the universal Church goes, the laity can now exert influence only through a few charismatic leaders or indirectly through writers and journalists. In short, Vatican II seems to have had little impact on the Church's central administration in Rome regarding matters of lay ecclesial responsibility.

On a diocesan level the Church has benefited from the dedicated commitment to the Council of a good number of bishops. Laity now actively participate in pastoral councils and are lay administrators of diocesan offices of social services, education, Catholic charities, youth and family ministries, and so on. They head diocesan papers and assume leadership roles as presidents of parish councils, as directors of religious education, youth services, and liturgy, and they even work on the staffs of many diocesan marriage tribunals and education offices.

However, even in those dioceses committed to reform, several serious structural and authority problems still jeopardize the development of serious lay ecclesial responsibility. Laity work in diocesan and parish councils, but they rarely have any real power.[7] Generally, they work under the possible veto power of a priests' council or local pastor. In fact, their pastor could be uninfluenced by Vatican II or even publicly opposed to it and yet still be allowed to exercise authority and control over laity attuned to the Council's message. Laity still have no rights or effective say in electing their pastor, and in most cases there is no evaluation of his pastoral performance. He may be incompetent, but they have no control. Or he may be excellent but may be removed without their input and replaced with someone dedicated to undoing his work.[8] If laity feel obliged to oppose the newcomer, there is generally no grievance machinery, no due process, and no lobbying ability. Canon 221 of the new Code assures due process to all, but the positive contributions of the Code will need to be made concrete in local Churches.[9]

The laity, then, participate less in the structures of today's Church than they do in those of civic life.[10] Yet, since human maturity demands a relationship on equal terms, it is desirable that we see all service and all authority as mutual. Laity in many dioceses and parishes are still treated as clients, and when they try to be more than silent sheep, they are reminded of the divine institution of the hierarchy and its authority.[11] Many priests, of course, handle the situation with prudence and understanding. But authority is at times exercised by newly ordained men, not much older than college graduates, who are placed over men and women with many years of study, experience, and commitment. "... the clergy, however inexperienced, can always exert their prerogatives as ordained persons, and there is nothing in Church law to prevent it."[12] While some Church leaders often give the impression that their main concern is to defend its institutional structures,[13] such defensiveness is simply not a priority for laity. One research study concludes:

> Lay influence in the Catholic Church in years ahead will exert continual pressure . . . away from the institutional model. . . . Lay influence in years ahead will favor movement toward democratization and away from hierarchical authority.[14]

We can also find encouragement in the trend toward recognizing the differences between authority instituted by Christ and the structures through which that authority is exercised.

Present structures are not only unacceptable from the perspective of ecclesiology; they are also apostolically inefficient and spiritually damaging. All over the country, competent and highly qualified laity are losing or leaving their jobs because of clashes with clerics who feel threatened. Many of these lay ecclesial ministers will, unfortunately, never return.

Much needs to be done, then, in the area of structures and authority. Karl Rahner, speaking of the shape of the Church to come, describes a Church from the roots, a democratized Church. He goes on to address the possibility of a declericalized Church:

The Church of the future must grow in its reality quite differently from the past, from below, from groups of those who have come to believe as a result of their own free, personal decision.[15]

In this Church to come, office will still be part of our community. In fact, Rahner claims it will be enhanced. But it will also need to be restricted. Such areas as administration, policy decisions, educational techniques, goal planning, financial management, and youth ministry are not part of the grace of the sacrament of orders. Clerical leaders have no protection against serious mistakes in these areas.[16] Much development has taken place in integrating laity, but many areas of the Church remain unchanged.

Rights and duties

Papal documents since the turn of the century have been a major force in Christian education to justice. A complementary flood of documents from Vatican offices and local hierarchies have also come out in support of social justice and human rights. But more and more we are realizing that what is presented to those outside the Church must become a reality for those inside the Church. Bishop James Niedergeses expressed well this type of concern:

There is a desperate need in the church for structures and procedures of which people are aware and from which they derive assurance of fairness and a place of respect in the assembly of God's people.[17]

If laity are to accept ecclesial responsibility, they must also be convinced that they will be treated justly and that their basic rights will be respected. In recent years the Church has been justly criticized for violating human rights in such areas as employment, right to privacy, sexual equality, and freedom of conscience. Some laity now see their ministry as a call to challenge the unjust corporation of the Church.[18] One of the most powerful condemnations of recent times was that of Rahner in his open letter to Cardinal Ratzinger:

The average Christian often has the bitter impression that his faith-inspired loyalty to the church is abused. And yet, he knows that he is powerless before the law. In [civil] society in such a case one can legitimately revolt against such misused power. But not so for the believing Christian. We can truly say that sensitivity to basic human rights must still develop within the church.[19]

Several local bishops have recently made major contributions toward rectifying this situation.[20] Most dioceses seem to be hoping that attitudes toward the laity's rights and duties will change and that appropriate structures will help so that a specific bill of rights will not need to be explicitly formulated. Bishop Cosgrove synthesized the following possibilities: "Rights are protected in many ways. Indirectly they are protected by education, growth of moral consciousness and development of character; directly they are protected by law."[21] Although much has been done indirectly by selfless and sensitive priests and bishops, more is required for the Church to continue to speak out boldly on rights. Increasingly, people are insisting that the Church publicly recognize specific rights. Perhaps the best listing of rights in recent months is that of Bishop Cosgrove:

- The right and freedom to hear the word of God and to participate in the sacramental and liturgical life of the church;
- The right and freedom to exercise the apostolate and share in the mission of the church;
- The right and freedom to speak and be heard and to receive objective information regarding the pastoral needs and affairs of the church;
- The right to education, to freedom of inquiry and to freedom of expression in the sacred sciences;
- The right to free assembly and association in the church;
- And such inviolable and universal rights of the human person as the right to the protection of one's

reputation, to respect of one's person, to activity in accord with the upright norm of one's conscience, to protection of privacy.[22]

To this list of basic rights, theologians have added others. Regarding the Church's mission, they say, laity have the right to preach. Regarding Church government, laity have the right to participate in ecclesiastical government, to depose pastors for justified grievances, to participate in councils of administration, to carry out such ecclesiastical functions as those of a judge, and to administer Church property.[23] After research, another author suggested that the lay right to participate in choosing ministers is "a permanent ecclesial category."[24]

One could also add the right that more will not be demanded of the layperson than is demanded of the cleric. Nevertheless, in a time of increasing demands for qualifications, certification, and updating for ministry, there are tendencies to demand of laity more in studies and training than is demanded of many clerics. Other rights would be a lived acceptance of the *sensus fidelium* (consensus of the faithful) and of real collegial forms of government. Collegial government should include the right to be consulted and actively involved in decision making and policy. This will imply the development of appropriate structures to allow lay participation in local diocesan meetings as a balance to clergy conferences, meetings, and informal clergy gatherings where much is often achieved but where laity are absent.[25] It will also imply more open financial records and lay participation in decisions on financial priorities. Finally, one should add the right of laity to receive respect and Christian love when they dissent. In post-Council years, dissent has frequently been equated with disloyalty. Actually, though, the *absence* of dissent can be disloyalty. Dissent is the beginning of a reflective process in noninfallible teaching. If we exclude the possibility of such dissent, we are taking a magical approach to Church authority.[26]

We can certainly be hopeful that the issue of lay rights will take a new direction in the years ahead as a result of the unprecedented list of rights in the newly revised Code of Canon Law. Canons 208-223 list the rights common to all the baptized, and Canons 224-231 deal specifically with the rights of laity. To these could be added Canons 298, 299, and 321-329, which deal with laity's rights to form associations.

Among the rights for laity specified in the above canons are the right to be treated with equality in accord with their condition and function, to be involved in evangelization, to make known their needs, to express their opinions regarding the good of the Church, to receive Word and sacraments, to found associations, to promote and sustain apostolic action, to receive Christian education, to enjoy freedom of inquiry; the right to freedom in civic life, to respect and privacy; the right to be installed in Church ministries and to receive suitable remuneration.

While it is encouraging to read this list of rights, the more serious questions will be how these rights will be interpreted and concretely applied on the local scene.

While the recognition and granting of the layperson's rights, including that of dissent, is crucial to the vitality of the Church today, the community of the Church should not become a battlefield for rights. Lay-rights or lay-liberation movements would be an unecclesial way to go, even though evangelical contestation and a little prophetical violence might help correct the injustice. However, a real sense of Church and an attitude of dialogue should be the chief means of enabling laity to assume their ecclesial responsibility with a confident awareness that they will be treated justly and fairly.

Collaboration within a common vision

The hallmark of the next decade must be the collaboration of all in the Church, both clergy and laity, in a common vision. It is necessary for the smooth running of new structures (L 26:1) and for parish development (L 10:2), but more particularly it is necessary in order to present the Church as the sacrament of unity for the world. To produce a collaboration based on mutual intervocational respect implies a true conversion. One author insightfully suggests: "The charism for now is communication leading to communion and made visible in community."[27]

The present fundamental problem—"the chasm that exists between clergy and lay people"[28]—is possibly one of the gravest crises in the entire history of the Church. Will lay liberation be willingly facilitated by a freeing Church, or will it be imposed on Church structures by lay-liberation movements? People from all walks of life hope that we will have the courage to be a freeing Church. Unfortunately, the persistence of pre-Council ecclesiology is discouraging. In 1972 David O'Brien, reflecting on the renewal of American Catholicism, expressed what are still real concerns:

> The lesson of history is clear: the Catholic Church preserved itself, its power and influence, at the cost of most of its dynamism and messianic drive. More than other institutions, the Church must fear not deviation but rigidity, not rebellious attempts to reach the reality behind itself but its own natural tendency to identify itself with that reality.[29]

In recent years, and especially in the speeches and actions of John Paul II, we have seen many signs that we must again fear rigidity. The pope's positions have been welcomed by many pre-Council churchgoing Catholics, both cleric and lay. But persons born or educated during or since the Council do not share the enthusiasm. In future decades only the second group will be alive. Dialogue and collaboration in a common vision must grow strong, must be based upon new, more flexible approaches to structures and authority, and must clearly recognize and respect mutual rights.

This collaboration in a common vision would not only affect structures and rights but would also be an experience of Church on which future theology could critically reflect. This collaboration among clergy, religious, and laity would not only sensitize laity to their ecclesial responsibility but could also help the laity have a healthier, more mature approach to the vocations of the priest and religious. Finally, this collaboration could result in a clearer definition of the vocation of the laity that would benefit not only laity but religious and clergy as well.

Laity and clerics could still collaborate principally in "the creation and effective operation of parish councils, diocesan pastoral councils, national pastoral councils, and [in] lay participation on various policy-making boards."[30]

These collaborative ventures would require serious preparation by both clerical and lay participants and would include ongoing theological education plus solid training in prayer and discernment. We have had enough business meetings in the Church and enough advice from management consultants. Our collaboration in a common vision must be a truly Christian experience—one based on scripture and Church documents, and carried out in prayerful dialogue, in addition to being rooted in the best of human experience. This kind of collaboration has been in evidence since the seventies, but laity have often been chosen for Church service because of their special competence in business administration, accounting, or plant management. Dedicated though these people have been, they have frequently lacked even an elementary background in contemporary ecclesiology, which is necessary for genuine ecclesial service in the Church. Priests have often been practical and businesslike, but some have had no sense of the vision of the Church. Collaboration in ecclesial responsibility is still essential, but it needs to be well prepared for and entered into with serious Christian commitment.

Lay Spiritual Life and Growth

Post-conciliar spiritual renewal

Throughout its history the Church has witnessed many periods of spiritual renewal in which laity have responded to the evangelical call to an ongoing conversion.[31] The years since Vatican II certainly have been such a period. Within local churches we have experienced strong lay commitment to liturgical participation and in general a willing adaptation to sacramental and ritual changes. Our people have welcomed parish renewal projects and have responded generously, often at great sacrifice, to the world's material needs. Many laity have shared in Church renewal by participating in the spiritual movements found in every country.[32] Some of these movements have even been started by laity—for example the Focolare, or earlier, the Legion of Mary. Lay participation in the charismatic movement and in prayer movements in general has had an exceptionally great impact. And social involvement movements or such family renewal movements as Marriage Encounter have developed and expanded. These same years have witnessed the growth of many spontaneous groups. Some put a heavy stress on community, as is seen in the basic ecclesial communities; some enrich other aspects of the Christian life-style, as is seen in prayer groups or faith-sharing groups.

All this has been good both for individual laity and for the universal Church. However, some significant weaknesses in recent renewal efforts could jeopardize serious in-depth renewal of the life and mission of laity. For one, the greater part of spiritual renewal in prayer and faith sharing has occurred outside of parish life in spontaneous groups and spiritual movements. This can be religiously and psychologically unhealthy, since many persons who have been educated in the centrality of the parish now find it disturbing that spiritual life and enrichment are fostered principally elsewhere today.

Another weakness is that liturgies are not only clerical in their leadership but also in style, tone, emphasis, and teaching. Again, the fact that most laity can readily manage without the sacraments for months at a time indicates that much lay spiritual renewal has not been sacramental.

An additional weakness is that the old ritual symbols, which have been doctored up to seem relevant to the modern world view—as have the minor orders and sacrament of reconciliation—simply have little meaning today.

Yet another weakness is that most laity, stunned by the failure to find true Christian community in their local parishes, have found spiritual life in movements and groups which at times have been elitist and not ecclesially centered—for instance, some of the non-parish-based spiritual movements.[33] Some laity have moved in religious commitment from one spiritual movement to another or have even belonged to several at the same time, in what can only be described as spiritual consumerism.

Those laity who do not belong to spiritual movements have met other obstacles in their path to spiritual renewal. Much of the written material being used for spiritual nourishment is a journalistic popularization of spirituality; and, as could be expected, a spirituality without good theological roots has become devotionalism. Some of the more recent serious theological works for laity are merely modern translations of pre-Vatican II books—but it is not possible to build a new and relevant spirituality on an old ecclesiology.[34]

Incarnational spirituality

In recent years new ways of thinking about spirituality have emerged. Christians desire to express their commitment in more vital and concrete ways. The classical spiritual problems of the past, such as the debate over grace between the Jesuits and Dominicans, are now not even considered. Rather, the concern is to show how Christian spirituality should be a response to the problems of today. As a result, modern spirituality is characterized more by the positive integration of human and religious values than by emphasis on one or other of the component parts of spiritual growth such as humility or prayer. It is characterized more by personal and spontaneous expressions of religious devotion and commitment as a manifestation of authentic self-development than by the repetition of formal methods established in the past. It is characterized more by a global vision and a sense of world responsibility than by self-examination and personal analysis. Today, spirituality is centered more on the person and on vital human needs and is determined very much by the concrete circumstances of our own age. The simplification of spiritual life in methods of prayer, forms of penance, styles of liturgy, and so on, and the positive attitude to world values are certainly two of the modern developments in spirituality that have great implications for laity. We now have a spirituality of presence to the world, a spirituality of incarnation. Holiness is seen to be specified by one's condition in life, and laity living in the midst of everyday world events, family, politics, finance, sexual growth, parenthood, and work are called to holiness precisely in these conditions. The document for laity in the Vatican Council expressed this well.

> The layman's religious program of life should take its special quality from his status as a married man and a family man, or as one who is unmarried or widowed, from his state of health, and from his professional and social activity.[35]

This spirituality of insertion and Christian presence in daily life and development of world values has been a healthy movement for laity. It draws into Christian significance the major components of lay life, long seen as excluding an atmosphere conducive to holiness.

Generally, however, there is a time lag between insights into spirituality and integration of these into daily life. Major Church issues still often seem irrelevant and meaningless to laypersons. Much preaching still presents a prepackaged and recycled spirituality from past religious practices—a spirituality that has not integrated the incarnational dimension and hence is often not applicable to the real needs of the laity. In spite of the theology of earthly realities, we still hear preaching that uses scripture to support an Augustinian-based dualism that sees matter and spirit as two opposing forces of life and considers the former as always evil. The frequent equating of sin with sexual immorality, and the absence of a spirituality of sexual growth, are indications that an incarnational approach is not yet a reality in the call to lay holiness. Again, the rat race in which laity find themselves has not been given a theological interpretation and challenge. The relationship between hectic living and spiritual growth has not been sufficiently examined, and the use of free time, leisure, and early retirement is a part of the lay condition that has not received the leavening influence of incarnational spirituality.

Today it is also crucial that we consider all our dealings with the world and society in the light of Christian spirituality. John Paul II speaks of the impact and challenge of the state of the world, while Brother David Steindl-Rast, reflecting on how we learn from the world around us, speaks of the "environment as guru."[36] The world today is in constant flux, and laity must creatively and spiritually deal with this change.[37] These attitudes toward their world are difficult for people who have been trained to despise the world and to commit themselves to unchanging truths in an unchanging Church.

Lay spirituality

The universal call to holiness proclaimed by Jesus and reaffirmed by the Vatican Council has in practice often eluded even the most dedicated spiritual leaders of the Church. We really do not have a spirituality of all the baptized, but a presumed state of perfection (the clerical or religious state) which is then presented in modified form to everyone else (the laity). We have already seen how even the most inexperienced young man, once ordained, is presumed to have authority and religious leadership he really may not possess. In general, forms of spiritual life and growth stages in prayer come from religious life. Spiritual direction often uses methods and styles appropriate for religious. Most retreat experiences are expensive, non-lay luxuries, and are at best modified versions of experiences in the lives of religious. Mystical prayer has been presumed to be reserved for contemplative and celibate religious, and their mysticism often portrays a celibate's sublimation of sexual need. We do not have a lay mysticism.

Some 81 percent of the canonized saints are clerical and religious. Of the 19 percent who are lay, "neither virgin nor martyr," as the missal so negatively labels them, many seem to have been canonized for supporting ecclesiastical positions.[38] If saints are our models of success, then the lay life seems a spiritual failure when judged by canonization statistics. Yet the small numbers of canonized lay saints may be due in large part to the fact that lay persons have no effective way of lobbying and no say in how their financial contributions are used.

This ecclesiastically dispensed spirituality is an unhealthy form of spiritual discrimination. After two thousand years, where are the lay saints canonized for their integration of Christianity and work, or of prayer and politics? Who are the lay models of conjugal love, of family life, of civic service? Who are the examples of a mature collaboration with the hierarchy, and who are the models of a healthy challenge and confrontation of the misuse of ecclesiastical authority?

The Vatican Council is the great modern call for the universality of commitment. Among the many spiritually significant teachings of Vatican II, the following can be highlighted: the focus on baptismal spirituality; the call of all Christians to quality prayer, to liturgical participation, and to ecclesial dedication; the forceful challenging of all baptized persons to involve themselves in ministry. Teachings like these make this generation very special for laity. The call has never been clearer, but there remain many obstacles to achieving it. With God-given liberty, laity must shed ecclesiastical management of spirituality and creatively explore a spirituality for all the baptized, not a spirituality derived from clerics or religious.

Laity: Mission and Ministry

The Vatican Council was not only a great theological

redirecting of the Church but also an ecclesial conversion in three major phases. In the years of the Council, the Church became aware of itself first of all as a community, then as a community living in the heart of the world, and finally as a community in the heart of the world in order to minister to the world. Community, incarnation, and ministry, then, are three conciliar insights that the Council universally applies to all the baptized. All Christians are life-giving members of this community. Called to be sacrament of the world in the circumstances of their own lives, they are challenged to mission and ministry as a necessary part of their baptismal commitment.

A generation's approaches to mission and ministry are the clearest indication of its ecclesiology, and post-conciliar efforts in this sphere are certainly indicative of a striving toward a new image of the Church.[39] Although this increase in the Church's self-understanding is being achieved with considerable pain and frustration, it is also an encouraging sign of hope and fidelity.

Ecclesial vision

As Vatican II proclaimed, the layperson is "a living instrument of the mission of the Church herself." Because of his or her union with Christ, the layperson has the right and duty to be involved in the ministry of the Church, both as an individual and as a member of organized groups.[40] Laity's charismatic gifts are in the Church for the good of others and must be identified and used.[41] These general principles of Vatican II have opened new avenues of involvement for laity in evangelization,[42] family ministries,[43] social development,[44] world transformation,[45] and internal Church life.[46]

Lay ministry is an ambiguous term that can be understood in at least three ways. In the broad sense it refers to Christian witness. While a broad use of the concept is valuable, the ministry obligations imposed on all at baptism include more than a general witnessing by a good life. When used in this first sense, the term is so broad it lacks real power. Evangelization is everyone's responsibility, and it implies life, word, and action on behalf of the Church.[47]

Sometimes *lay ministry* refers to volunteer work undertaken as an extra. But that understanding seems to divide the committed laity from the mediocre. These part-time ministries can be spontaneous or ecclesiastically organized. Spontaneous ministries, as in some prayer groups and social-justice work, have sometimes developed excesses and led to polarization, and as a result Church leaders have tried to oversee even these ministries in whatever way possible. This supervision can guarantee the ecclesial character of all ministry, but it can also amount to an unhealthy ecclesiastical control over ministry that leads to a poor ecclesiology implying that ecclesiastical authorization is needed for every ministry.

Rather than speak of part-time ministry, it would be better to speak of a permanent commitment to ministry that results from baptism and that can be exercised in either full-time or part-time service. But how do we authenticate or officially recognize the various lay ministries without institutionalizing the charism? Is Church leadership intended to assist, or to regulate? to cooperate, or to delegate? Too often, ecclesial acceptance has been confused with ecclesiastical acceptance. The former is always necessary; the latter is not.

Whatever ministry a person is involved in is a ministry of the Church, because every baptized Christian carries out the mission of the Church. Frequently, fellow Christians confirm one another in ministry, as when married couples use the services of other married couples to solve family problems, or when parents entrust their child's education to a teacher, or when neighbors identify a friend as good in prayer training. At no time in these cases is it necessary to have an official Church authorization; what is needed, rather, is the call and authorization of fellow members of the Church. Ecclesiastical acceptance is not always necessary, but ecclesial acceptance is.

Finally, *lay minister* is used to identify the full-time

professional lay person whose services to the local Church are either paid or volunteer. Some authors have recommended a quasi-ordination for such people as a step toward declericalizating ministries.[48] But this would simply put another rung on the hierarchical ladder.

The full-time professional layperson received support in his or her commitment from John Paul II, who also warned of future difficulties in the area of role clarification.[49] The U.S. bishops also welcomed this development of full-time lay ministry, but they insisted that "all such ministries must be recognized by the community and authenticated by it in the person of its leader."[50] Unfortunately, this practice has often thwarted baptismal equality and promoted the growth of an employer-employee relationship in which the employer not only hires but also claims special divine guidance and sacramental grace to teach, govern, and sanctify. Another difficulty is that full-time lay ecclesial ministers have, like the priests, given years of their life to training but, unlike the priests, have had to finance it themselves. Moreover, as has been mentioned, after ordination the priest gets automatic placement irrespective of competence; the lay minister often lacks placement even though very well qualified.

Linked to this problem is the fact that the process of official formal acceptance of laity into Church-sponsored ministries needs to be clarified and possibly a national procedure established. However, any evaluation of the lay minister's pastoral performance would be appropriate only when there is also a process of ongoing evaluation of the pastoral performance of the clergy. Robert Kinast, commenting on this whole problem, suggests:

> The guiding concern is not who is superior, who makes final decisions, who judges the acceptability of charisms but rather how may laity and clergy free each other so that together they may be a more liberating force.[51]

This collaboration often does not exist, and a fellow contributor with Kinast sadly admits:

The giving of *per*mission is much more frequently used than the giving of *mission*. Bishops and pastors hire, draft, appoint, delegate, permit and mandate. They authorize, place and assign. They allocate and dispense.[52]

But despite all the problems involved, the integration of the layperson into the mission of the Church is under way with powerful support from all areas of the Church. The pope, bishops, priests, religious, and laity are committed to facilitating ministry in laity. This is unquestionably one of the great signs of life in the Church of our times.

Shared responsibility

The variety of ministries established by the Lord must be preserved or reintroduced where they have fallen into disuse. Laity must not be deprived of those ministries that are a necessary fulfillment of their baptismal responsibilities.[53] In this generation, part of the call of priests and religious is to facilitate the development of lay ministry and shared ministry.[54] In fact, as the Vatican Council stated, all approaches to the Church are partial without a shared responsibility in ministry.

The Church has not been truly established, and is not yet fully alive, nor is it a perfect sign of Christ among men, unless there exists a laity worthy of the name working along with the hierarchy.[55]

Such shared responsibility requires that each baptized Christian be guaranteed not only freedom in the responsible involvement in ministry but also freedom of speech regarding what he or she judges to be best for the Church.[56] This collaboration demands of all a common vision, humility, and confidence in the Lord's supportive presence.[57]

Since the Council we have seen exceptional efforts toward sharing responsibility for the mission of the Church. Vision, guidance, and challenge have come from many directions,[58] and new areas of shared responsibility have developed.[59] We have witnessed the growth of specialization in ministry, mobile inter-parish ministry, team ministry, and intervocational ministry. Dioceses and parishes have been restructured to foster and manifest shared responsibility, and volunteer laity have been drawn into such ministries as education, social services, and community building. Other laity, as we saw in Chapter 1, have felt free to explore new and creative approaches to ministry, and in many cases they have been welcomed and supported in their discoveries.

However, the whole area of lay ministry and shared ministry is like a beautiful meadow that is also a mine field. Shared responsibility is especially difficult "where one person—willingly or unwillingly—represents the 'establishment' and another stands for the 'new breed.'"[60] We still have far too much emphasis on ecclesiastical jurisdiction and far too little consideration of charisms. Where this is true we have only a theory of shared responsibility, not the practice of it. In such cases we have only the outmoded concept that the laity have no real ministry of their own but are merely mandated to participate in the hierarchy's mission. One priest shares his honest reflections:

> I think that for many of us, despite the documents of Vatican II and the theology we have studied and professed, there is a deep down feeling which says that "true ministry" is really mine. It is really what I, the priest, do. And if others are allowed at all to share in this ministry it is first of all by necessity, secondly by delegation, and finally, strictly a temporary matter.[61]

Talk about lay ministry often presumes that it is the priest who is sharing his responsibility with the laity. Even in shared ministry the layperson becomes the object of a clerical apostolate, either sharing in the priest's tasks or being commissioned to work in spheres where the clergy, and later the religious, have not had success.[62] In this approach laity are reduced to being an extended arm of the hierarchy. One author expresses well a common reaction to this position:

> Other ministries should be understood not merely as a

sharing or a substitute for the ordained ministry. It is not that ministries exist because they are recognized by ordained ministers. It is because ministries exist that they should be recognized.[63]

When shared responsibility is applied in areas where laity are hired full-time for Church needs, other problems arise. Laity are hired because of competence, but they have no real authority. They receive delegated accountability to the pastor, who has veto power over the layperson. The laity's ministry is generally task-oriented, with little involvement in pastoral planning or policy, which is frequently reserved to a "spiritual level." Although laypersons are hired for their competence, job security does not depend on competence but on the whim of the pastor. If federal laws on equal opportunity employment and the hiring of minorities were applied to the Church, there would be grounds for an endless stream of court cases.[64]

Since the Church's most important ministry is to live in unity, it is crucial that we overcome these difficulties. Otherwise the exodus of the best will continue, or laypersons will continue to dedicate themselves to non-ecclesiastically-controlled ministries.

Problems for ministry

In one of his addresses to lay Church workers, Pope John Paul II anticipated several problems of laity in ministry but urged all lay ministers to persevere through this period of painful growth.

> Hold fast to this [commitment], even if further clarification of your calling's form will still require reflection. If you do not receive from everyone in the communities that acceptance and welcome which you have so far experienced and which you have hoped for, it seems important to me that you should go on intelligently in hard situations above all, and remind yourselves of the idealism of your beginnings and try to win

over other collaborators and communities gradually. We all believe that one and the same Spirit, who guides the communities and hearts of men, has summoned your service in the church into life. You are called to entrust yourselves to this Spirit precisely when faced with trouble.[65]

The pope speaks of the need to further clarify the layperson's calling. This will take time, research, and collaboration. However, many bishops are already voicing concern over what they see as the limited focus of lay ministry. While lay involvement in the life and organization of the Church is growing, the bishops feel that the absence of Catholic lay involvement in the working world is "the single biggest problem facing the U.S. Church."[66] Bishop John L. May of Mobile, Alabama, goes even further in criticizing the misdirection of lay ministry: "In some areas, such as labor-management, politics and higher education, Catholic laity are now exerting less leadership than before the council."[67]

From the times of the Council (and before), laity have been challenged to bring a Christian spirit to the environment in which they live,[68] and many lay associations have successfully done this.[69] The bishops' concern remains a serious issue to address, since the Church is not a sacrament to itself but a sacrament for the world.

Perhaps the Church could look into the possibility of giving concrete financial aid to support lay ministries of social involvement. Some religious communities in America today have an annual budget of over $250,000 to promote vocations. Every diocese has money set aside for vocation development, either directly in promotion and marketing, or indirectly in salaries for vocation directors. Nowadays it costs about $17,000 a year to train each seminarian, even though many seminarians do not arrive at ordination. If these costs for clerical ministry were totaled for the United States alone, the figure would be shocking. It would also be extremely difficult to find many people who believe this money is well spent. Why should the laity's money be used exclusively by clerics to promote clerical ministry? Many dioceses know for certain that if present trends continue, they cannot cope with their ministry needs after the nineties. The long-term solution is a rethinking of the nature of the priesthood, but the short-term solution is to invest more heavily in lay ministry. When we pray for vocations and when dioceses budget for vocation recruitment, we must all use a broader concept of vocation.

As well as recognizing the need to clarify the layperson's calling, the pope also refers to the need for acceptance of lay ministry. Many are slow to accept a lay leader, especially in spiritual areas.[70] A leadership role of a cleric or religious is passed on automatically to the succeeding cleric or religious but not to a layperson; each layperson must prove himself or herself. Yet role modeling, not competence, is the main short-run criterion, and this has often led laypersons to mimic the cleric in an undoubtedly subconscious effort to attain job security.

Suzanne Elsesser, in her address to the Fourth Annual Conference of Lay Ministry Coordinators, suggested several ways to enhance the acceptance of ecclesial ministers.[71] All persons involved need patience; the ministers need a clear view of their roles; the people need to experience the competence of the lay leader; the Church needs to give supportive official action; and all need continuing education. We cannot afford to turn lay leaders into functionaries or project directors but must assure them of acceptance and welcome, believing with the pope that the Spirit has called for their service in the Church.

Another problem facing lay ministry today is the lack of support structures. Religious have their communities; priests have the priests' senate and the presbyterate; but laity have no ministry structure to support, inspire, and challenge them. They can become frustrated, their work routine,[72] their ministry merely a job.[73] Often, financing comes from parishes, not dioceses, and so it is the parish that controls the lay minister and lay ministry. Diocesan support structures are difficult to establish for specific functions when each lay minister's job description is parish-based.

Often we have no diocesan image of the various lay ministries.

Then there is the problem of finance. The budget cutbacks of recent years have led parishes and dioceses to lay off excellent lay ministers. Commitment to developing support structures is all the more urgent in this atmosphere. Elsesser calls for support structures to strengthen lay ministers' commitment and to contribute to their ongoing education and formation. She insists they are necessary for recruitment, placement, and accreditation.[74]

In addition, support structures would help ease the problem of work stress in ministry. Burnout in full-time lay ministers is now high, and many laypersons opt out of volunteer work. Establishing support structures for the ongoing development of prayer, theological training, and social awareness is crucial.

A further problem area that needs attention is the Church's employment practices.[75] I have referred to the lack of job descriptions, or worse still, the multiplicity of job descriptions within the same local Church.[76] Many laity rightly see their work in education and social service as ministry but feel they are cheap labor for the Church. In most publicized cases throughout the nation—for example, those of teachers in Catholic schools—laity have even been denied the basic right to organize and bargain collectively. The teachings of the universal Church and of the U.S. bishops clearly support their right. And yet Thomas J. Lynch, in his address to the Canon Law Society of America, claims that Church teaching on this point is not practiced by many dioceses in the U.S. Where problems have arisen, he claims, Church groups have hired anti-union consulting firms, and he refers to seventy-one documented cases of Church reprisals against lay workers who tried to organize.[77]

Low salaries place the majority of full-time lay ministers below the U.S. poverty level. Even so, these ministers are frequently under the threat of competition from the even cheaper labor force of religious. For anyone who hopes for job security, fringe benefits, and good salary, lay ministry is not the place to be. Even for those who are willing to work hard, live simply, and rely on the providence of the Lord for their future, the advancement opportunities in the Church are practically nonexistent.

Despite many conflicts and problems, the whole development of lay ministry still heralds growth. The issue seems to be provoking an identity crisis for the Church in mission, but the opportunity for a creative response is challenging to many. We need an honest solution to the internal problems so that we can proclaim a message to the world with sincerity.

Some Pastoral and Theological Problems

Vatican Council II, in its document on the *Church Today*, concluded the section on the human community with an insightful challenge: "We can justly consider that the future of humanity lies in the hands of those who are strong enough to provide coming generations with reasons for living and hoping."[78]

What is seen as necessary for the whole human community is equally true of the Church, and developments in these post-Council years have certainly given the laity reasons for living and hoping. Developments in lay ministry during the last two decades can be viewed with a sense of satisfaction and hope insofar as they herald a new period of ecclesial life and can lead to genuine reform. These same recent events call for continued and profound changes in the Church. As we have already seen, ecclesial responsibility, spiritual life and growth, mission, and ministry will inevitably be lived differently in the years ahead, and this will lead to greater roles for laity. Certainly this is a period of hope.

Unfortunately there is much resistance to this change, as can be seen in the different priorities of hierarchy and laity; in the one-sided emphasis given to some teachings; and in the continuation of notable blind spots in the Church's life. The pastoral and theological implications of some recent

Church decisions and practices need to be evaluated and, when necessary, challenged, for they frequently contribute to the ongoing negative image of the layperson.

There are many signs of hope and some signs of frustration. When the latter seem so numerous and profound, Paul's words about his own ministry seem verified for the Church as a whole: "We are in difficulties on all sides, but never cornered; we see no answer to our problems, but never despair" (2 Co. 4:8).

Questionable priorities

Many Church priorities set by and for clerics are either not good for laity or are totally irrelevant to them. Notable among these is the seemingly overriding concern for structural permanence, even at the cost of suppressing the prophetical voice. When that voice becomes too strong to resist, concessions are reluctantly made. Even after all these centuries, the Church has not learned to be willingly attentive to "professional irritants." Absolutizing structures and being totally committed to their permanence are still among the social sins the Church shares with other multinational corporations. But sociological studies show that many laity, even the faithful and practicing members of the local Church, do not share this concern for maintaining structures at all cost.[79] To emphasize survival rather than reincarnation in a future-shock society is contrary to the very nature and mission of the Church as sacrament of the world. Those who comfortably wish to preserve the present situation are among the greatest enemies of the Church. Robert McAfee Brown likes to think of the Church as being on the frontiers of life. "A frontier situation, however, means to be adaptable and mobile—adaptable to new situations, and mobile to enter into yet newer situations."[80] Laity are forced to be adaptable and mobile in every aspect of their life except in the unchanging Church. Certainly since the Council we have witnessed many changes of practices in the Church but few profound changes in structures and self-understanding.

The disease of future-shock is also present in the Church as "a real sickness from which increasingly large numbers already suffer."[81] We need to sacrifice our attachment to structures and develop a new practical ecclesiology that gives priority to persons—which means to all the baptized.

> The prevailing structures and practices of the institutional Church are, with rare exceptions, not adapted to . . . [the] exercise of lay initiative, and need to be modified to allow for it.[82]

Laity are not primarily interested in clerical needs; this insistence on structural survival is the stifling priority of a few.

In his own time, Jesus condemned leaders "who make their authority felt" or "who lord it over others," and he insisted "it is not to be so with you" (Lk. 22:24-27). There is practically no organization in the world today where authority and obedience are so insisted upon as in the Church. Sadly, we all know of spiritual leaders who have given themselves to the service of the people but who "lord it over them" and "make their authority felt." James Walsh, reflecting on such situations, comments: "There is a fairly exact proportion between the defective administration of authority and the instinctive human reluctance to obey."[83] The emphasis on structures has led to selective disobedience, endless wrangling, and rupture of the community spirit of the Church. The human person, made in the image of God, is free, and the Church is the sacrament of freedom in which dissent and evangelical contestation are rights. But this freedom is not a recognizable priority of the Church. No one deserves immediate blame, for we are dealing with the education of decades. However, Thomas Lynch's words are valid here:

> There is simply no evidence that anyone in authority is trying deliberately to oppress people. But the happy lack of malice does not equal being right. It is always possible to harm others gravely through motives that are subjectively sincere but objectively wrong.[84]

Even though the situation may not be caused by malice, we are living in a clerically dominated Church, and this simply does not correspond to the nature of the Church. Unless this situation is changed, it will continue to be presumed that maintaining clerical dominance is a priority.

Not only must the structures of the Church be examined; clear goals at all levels must also be established. In spite of all the money spent on management consultants, and in spite of its clear mission, the Church is the largest organization in the world without goals. There is still a general aimlessness about the Church. In an effort to be faithful to a message that came in the past, we end up being faithful to the past itself. Laity know only images of the Church that come from the past, and their consciences are tranquilized by their fidelity to that past. This fosters conservatism. Edward Schillebeeckx speaks of "the world of past memory" and "the world of the future." The latter he identifies with dynamic humankind; the former he identifies with the Church.[85] The Church, however, must look forward in hope and offer images of the future.

Priorities of renewal have often been externals (like renovating the sanctuary), practices (like celebrating paraliturgies instead of reciting the rosary), and some procedures (like those in marriage cases), but not really essentials. It is significant that, on an ecumenical level, the Catholic Church shies away from the profound challenges of Protestantism and turns to the even more clerically dominated and ultraconservative Eastern Churches.

In addition to these problems related to Church structure, I have already referred to the questionable priorities seen in the allocation of Church resources, the lamentable past emphasis on information rather than on formation, and the concern with priestly and religious vocations rather than with the development of a challenging paradigm or image for the lay vocation. All these priorities block the healthy integration of laity into the Church.

One-sided teachings

Another major problem affecting laity is the uneven

emphasis on some truths in the Church without a balancing acknowledgment of others. Each period of history has its own tensions, and some teachings of the Church naturally tend to be more emphasized in one generation than in another. Selectivity in teachings, however, must be handled carefully and humbly; otherwise the teachings are not sources that lead to life but are means to defend already-accepted positions.

I have referred to a one-sided emphasis on lay obedience to the hierarchy without the complementary dimension of the hierarchy's obedience to the Spirit discerned in the people. Laity are trained to obey, but they are not deliberately trained "for genuine constructive criticism."[86] I have also indicated the unacceptability of a clerical authorization and mandate for laity without the parallel evaluation of the minister by the people. The one-sided spiritual leadership of males without female leadership is also unhealthy. The strong proclamation of the vocation to the ministerial priesthood without an adequate formulation of the doctrine of the priesthood of all the baptized is yet another example of incomplete and one-sided teaching that does injustice to laity.[87]

Incomplete or one-sided approaches to teachings generally lead to exaggerations that harm the Church. The Church is not only institution but mystery; not only hierarchical but collegial. We need both office and charism, obedience and co-responsibility, flight from the world and involvement in it. Both sides of each truth should be taught.

In addition to the frequent lack of such a balanced teaching, it is difficult at times to distinguish between a teaching and its outward form. The former is permanent; the latter is not. We must believe the teaching, but we can discard the form over time. The formulation of doctrine is conditioned by the time of its origin. Unfortunately, laity are called to believe in the forms of the dogmas and not just in the dogmas themselves. Cases in point are papal infallibility and the Marian dogmas.[88]

There is the additional difficulty of the Church's

unconsciously misleading laity to believe that some recently developed teaching came from Jesus. The present roles of bishops and pope are examples of this.[89]

Another problem arises at times when the Church puts pressure on laity by presenting only one ethical interpretation of an issue. At times we have a sort of ethical and juridical colonialism in the Church when local leaders pastorally pressure gullible laity into their ethical fold. There are many models of ethical behavior today, and it is unjust to present only one model when others are also common among scholars. For instance, to insist that morality be determined by a theory of natural law within us all, when large numbers of ethicists and social scientists reject such a theory, is itself unethical. Such ethical selectivism can also be manifested in a kind of hierarchy of guilt. To reprove a couple who are lax in sexual matters but to ignore the unjust way they manage their business is false teaching.[90]

Sometimes one-sided teachings are traceable to clerical ignorance; clerics present only one side of teaching because frequently they have not studied the issue in depth. For instance, originally it was normal for laity to preach. Now we have religious reasons why they should not! What is the historical development of this newer position, and why must it be rejected?[91] It is also generally accepted now that there were several models of Church government in New Testament times, but only one is presented today. The refusal by Church leaders to address these issues because of a lack of openness or study seriously limits Church growth. Moreover, some Church leaders operate out of a theology that does not allow them to accept the changes needed today, and they impose their theology on the laity. This deductive, magisterial, downward method of teaching is detrimental to laity and to the whole Church. The problem is intensified when we have a literalist and fundamentalist approach to Church documents and teachings—an approach that takes every word at face value without appreciating the background, history, and politics that produced it. Leaders must show much greater sensitivity in listening to the teachings inductively arrived at from all the baptized.

Other problem areas

In addition to reordering its priorities and taking a balanced approach to its teachings, the Church must become aware of several new developments since the Council. Roman Catholicism today is no longer a unified Church. There are several subgroups, each with its own theology, reasoned arguments, style of life, and forms of worship. There are middle-of-the-road groups, conservatives, liberals, ultra-conservatives and ultra-liberals, or whatever names seem suitable.

These same structural divisions are present in other Christian churches, too. This is not true pluralism, for there is no effort at unity, and where such pluralism does not strive for unity, it is hardly Christian. Members of these subdivisions at times feel more at home with members of the same sub-group in another church; there is more communion across ecumenical lines than within the churches. We have not only a structural diffusion within the various churches, where each church is divided into subgroups, but a new structural realignment where subgroups of like mind from different churches then organize together. This is supported at times by a variety of liturgies in the same parish, and by all kinds of sharing groups. This "cafeteria" approach to Church life will grow in the years ahead as laity with new-found freedom, but without appropriate guidance, explore their own ways of being Church. This approach threatens the community and unity of the Church and should be challenged.

Another area that needs to be looked at carefully is the class system of the Church. For a long time the cleric was prime, but the "Vatican council would be described as the declericalization of the Catholic Church."[92] Unfortunately, many now have a negative approach to the priest, and nowadays most parents do not want their sons to become priests. Rather, today we run the risk of new classes of

Christians who are involved in ministry or who belong to the spiritual movements. We frequently hear: "I'm an ecclesial minister," "I'm a pastoral associate," "I'm a charismatic," "I'm a cursillista." Many laity who are deeply involved with the Church become clerical in their style. Soon after the Council this possibility was lamented:

> What bothers me is that I think I see signs of a caste-system developing among the laity, the emergence of a kind of pseudo-hierarchy of professional laymen whose mind-set frequently is dismayingly clerical and whose preoccupations are overwhelmingly ecclesiastical in the narrow sense.[93]

A third area, and one to which we have seemingly closed our eyes, is the increasing number of marginal Christians who think of themselves as believers but who have opted out of structured Church. This is typical of the middle class who go their own way, do their own thing, and are convinced that "God understands me." They take what they like and leave what they dislike. The result is constant compromise that does not renew, and the firm communication barriers prevent challenge from the outside.

Other blind spots for laity include the overburdening of their priests, the burnout of the religious, the laity's increasing lack of religious education, and the persistent absence of social involvement. Above all, there is an absence of in-depth change while laity often manifest an adolescent optimism about superficial developments. Ironically, with the increase of lay ministry in Church positions, we run the risk of diminishing lay transformation of the world.

Conclusion

In this chapter we have surveyed developments since the Council in the life and role of the layperson in the Catholic Church. We reviewed the Church's sense of the laity's ecclesial responsibility; evaluated developments in the laity's spiritual life and growth; examined the Church's acceptance of lay mission and ministry; and indicated some relevant pastoral and theological problems.

Some identifiable lay attitudes today are profoundly different from any found in the past. These could lead to the creative reinterpretation of Christianity and give a new direction to the Church of tomorrow.[94] The problems we need to confront are overwhelming to many, and others have lost confidence that some Church leaders will ever respond to the Church's and the world's common needs. The official Church's return to conservatism and its lack of flexibility seem to manifest a lack of faith in Christianity's relevance to the eighties. If this century closes without the Church's having capitalized on lay life, it will be one of the tragedies of Church history.

Renewal never comes through edict but only by participation. We need to see creativity in ecclesial life-styles and responsibility. In this the laity have much experience to share.[95] The problems should not paralyze us; in fact, if we work through them, renewal will be within our grasp. One writer insightfully suggests:

> Paradoxically, only out of the institutional and intellectual chaos such as present Catholicism is experiencing, could an authentic revival of Catholicism occur, and an authentic Catholic synthesis of modernity and the gospel be achieved.[96]

Some forms of the Church derive from the Jesus-event, but "an immense amount of the Church's shape comes also from the historical conditions."[97] We must, in fidelity to the Jesus-event, change the historical conditions; and there is no more crucial area of change than the life of the laity. Formerly the clergy-laity relationship was expressed in active-passive life, but if this continues, the organism is sick.

We live in a world and a Church of accelerated change. This is God's gift and promise. These years give us an opportunity to respond to the challenges, and we must do so because the stakes are high.

3

The Church as Family

Introduction

At the close of the Second Vatican Council in 1965, Paul VI said, "Now we begin to study the Church." Although there have been twenty-one ecumenical councils, no previous council had studied the Church in so much depth. Much of the Council's work was done under the direction and facilitation of Cardinal Montini, who as Paul VI succeeded John XXIII. In the Council Paul VI was a great reformer, but afterward he gradually became a hesitant compromiser. Nevertheless he remains one of the great initiators of ecclesial and ecclesiological reform in our generation. John Paul II could say of him, "Paul VI left us a witness of an extremely acute consciousness of the Church."[1]

In some ways it is possible to see the brief pontificate of John Paul I as a careful and delicate refocusing of what it means to be Church. We remember his love, concern, friendliness, openness, and spirit of welcoming. The impressions of his fatherliness and genuine Christian love were so strong, and he seemed to many to touch on such essentials that the cardinals, we are told, sought similar qualities in his successor. Many waited in vain for a policy statement from John Paul I. Others felt and believed that in his ecclesial living he had forcefully presented the great and perennial teachings on Christian life.

His successor has challenged us in many ways to deepen our awareness of what it means to be Church, with no challenge more forceful than the call in his first encyclical:

> The church's consciousness, enlightened and supported by the Holy Spirit and fathoming more and

more deeply both her divine mystery and her human mission, and even her human weakness—this consciousness is and must remain the first source of the church's love, as love in turn helps to strengthen and deepen her consciousness.[2]

The leadership of Paul VI, John Paul I, and John Paul II has been complemented by the growth in ecclesial awareness fostered by spiritual movements, theologians, and outstanding clergy, religious, and laity. The insights and renewal efforts of all are powerful manifestations of the guidance of the Holy Spirit in our times, and whenever one thinks of this, one also recalls the words of Christ: "Now I have opened in front of you a door which no one will ever close" (Rev. 3:8). The growth in awareness and the dedication to involvement in Church life have indeed opened a door that no one will ever close. But we need great courage to walk through this open door.

When Jesus began his work in Galilee, he proclaimed the Good News from God. "The time has come," he said, "and the kingdom of God is close at hand. Repent and believe the Good News" (Mk. 1:14-15). Since Jesus' first words, genuine conversion to the Good News has always been related to development of the life of the Church, but never have his words been so powerfully before our minds as they are today. Today's conversion, more than ever before, is a conversion to be Church; from all sides we are being called to an ongoing conversion to ecclesial life, and this implies a demanding asceticism for every one of us.

Church as the Family of God

The way we understand the Church conditions the way we live as Church. Some understandings of the Church leave nothing but a passive role to laity. Many portraits of the Church are presented in clerical and theological jargon and are very difficult to understand. Most conciliar and postconciliar models of the Church use exclusively theological and clerical concepts. Most laity today still understand the

Church as primarily a hierarchical and clerical organization, and when they are challenged to live as Church, they encounter the difficulty of integrating a lay life into a clerical understanding of Church.

Because there is a close relationship between the way we think of the Church and our commitment and involvement as Church, we must find a more vital model of the Church for our time. We must find a model that is understandable to laity; that has a lay dynamic in it; that calls for spirituality relevant to lay life; that portrays sufficiently the life and mission of laity; that integrates the role of laity into the whole life of the Church.

Getting to know the Church

Our search for a new model of the Church comes during a century remarkable in the whole history of ecclesiology. We have benefited from the great contributions of the biblical, liturgical, lay-apostolic, and ecumenical movements, all of which have had an impact on our understanding of the nature of the Church. We have seen a series of remarkable popes, beginning with Leo XIII, who have given new directions to the Church.[3] We have witnessed the birth and growth of spiritual movements in every country—movements that have aroused among the faithful a rededication to evangelical values. We have become accustomed to a grass-roots Christianity that demands to be heard. Above all, we have participated in the Second Vatican Council, in both the event and the aftermath.

Certainly, then, this is not a century of apathy and lack of interest in ecclesial matters; rather it is a period of growth in the Church's self-understanding and willingness to acknowledge crises and to deal with some of them. Theologians, reflecting on both the teachings of the times and the experience of the people, have presented more studies on ecclesiology than ever before.

Notable among these studies was a small but significant work of the American theologian Avery Dulles.[4] In his book, which he considers "a critical assessment of the Church in all its aspects," he directs his attention to the use of models in understanding the Church, and he describes how models develop. Since the Church is a great mystery that cannot be simply defined, we try to catch glimpses of its nature and purpose by using images taken from scripture or contemporary life. Now and again one or other of these images becomes more significant and evokes clearly defined responses in the faithful. As a result, these useful images become symbols of the Church and evoke what they symbolize. Even later, these symbols can dynamically develop our understanding of the Church, and a few can be "employed reflectively and critically to deepen one's theoretical understanding" of the Church.[5] Symbols such as these are called models. In each generation one model seems to surface and be embraced with great confidence; this model seems to be the commonly accepted way of understanding and explaining the Church. This prime model Dulles calls a paradigm.

Dulles gave five models of the Church that he thought important in the seventies: institution, mystical communion, sacrament, herald, servant. Less than a decade later, however, he considered all five unacceptable.[6]

In addition to Dulles' models, in the years since the Council we have heard, read, and studied about a variety of understandings of the Church: people of God, pilgrim people, chosen assembly, household of the Lord, mystical body of Christ, and total Christ. Theologians contributed other insights. Some saw, among other models, mission as the symbol for understanding the Church today; some viewed Trinitarian love as the ground of the Church.[7]

Some of these models are theologically powerful but pastorally impossible to deal with. Others have only limited use because their very mention gives rise to polemics. The common problem in all these models is that they are easily understandable only to the theologian or cleric. Even the simple concept of servant has many theological overtones. After all the efforts of these last two decades, no one model has become widely accepted. In fact, Dulles himself acknowledges:

> Of all the paradigms here considered, only the first—the institutional—corresponds to the common Roman Catholic experience of Church, but for many this image accents the very features they find least admirable and attractive.[8]

The one great advantage of the institutional model, in addition to history and tradition, is that it is understandable to laity who are daily immersed in institutions of every kind. The other models failed because of "excessive intellectualism" and elitism. They were not models for all the baptized, and they often focused on selective approaches to Church life.

Dulles recently evaluated the previous models and found them unsatisfactory. He then proposed a new understanding of the Church as a community of disciples.

> The discipleship model, by overcoming the excessive intellectualism of some other current conceptions, makes it clearer how every Christian can be called in some way to be a missionary.[9]

This recent model has several strengths, not least of which is its availability to all the baptized. While most other models are deduced from general Catholic principles,[10] the discipleship model seems to imply that the Church holds within its own members the very things that make it Church. This view of the Church as a community of disciples is valuable in relation to the roles of laity and their insights and contributions to our understanding of what it means to be Church.

However, even though Dulles has focused our considerations a little more, he has perhaps still not identified the prime model for today. Previously, he had stated:

> A model rises to the status of a paradigm when it has proved successful in solving a great variety of problems and is expected to be an appropriate tool for unraveling anomalies as yet unsolved.[11]

The discipleship model does not seem to meet these criteria. Moreover, it has been primarily used as an adjunct to other models such as the hierarchical one, and thus it can be interpreted in too many different ways.

It is difficult, then, to find the paradigm of our decade; one has apparently not yet surfaced, and we are still left with too many models. Clearly, though, the new direction for the future is to an understanding of the Church that is simple enough to be appreciated by all the baptized; is symbolic enough to evoke attitudes and courses of action; is clear enough to reflectively and critically deepen our theoretical understanding of the Church; is successful in responding to the problems of our time.

Though I have not found a paradigm for our decade, some common Church traits identifiable today may lead to one. Whether we look at the swings in theological development over recent years, at the common components of the spiritual movements, at the Council's experience and teaching, at the insights of theologians, or at the proclamations of Church leaders, there appears to be a consensus, a common ground leading to our identifying at least initial components of a unified vision.

The Church as family

All men and women are called to union with Christ (C 3:2); however, their call is not as individuals but as members of a community (CT 32:1). In fact:

> God has gathered together as one all those who in faith look upon Jesus as the author of salvation and the source of unity and peace, and has established them as the Church, that for each and all she may be the visible sacrament of this saving unity. (C 9:6)

Moreover, the word *Church* used in most of the North European languages comes from the Greek *kyriakē oikia,* "the family of the Lord." It is significant that when people sought a word to describe the reality of what it means to be

Church, the word they chose meant "family of the Lord."

The word *family* is also extensively used in ecclesiology, particularly in the documents of the Vatican Council, to describe both the Church as a whole and the local diocesan Church (C 32:5). The presbyterate is called a *family* (B 28:1); so, too, are the staff and students of a major seminary (PF 5:2), and of a minor seminary (PF 3). Religious are called to be a family (C 43:2), while religious orders are described as families (RL 1:2). Groups not juridically united but of a similar spirit are also called a family (RL 22), and local community living is modeled on the family (RL 15:1). It is clear, then, that everyone is called to live some dimension of a family spirituality. There is a strong spiritual interrelationship between ecclesial living and family living: They not only help each other, but they are necessary to each other. Omit one, and the other will suffer.

This image of the Church as family is ascetically and spiritually very challenging; moreover, it is much more easily understood than are many others. Besides, since the family is the basic experience of laity in their prime groups that make up the Church, this approach capitalizes on the laity's knowledge, experience, and contributions. This image also highlights the lay role, for not only does Vatican II see the Church as a family, but it also sees the family as a domestic Church. There is, in fact, a dynamic interrelationship between family life and Church life.

We read that the Church is a "fellowship of life, charity and truth" (C 9:5); "it is a people made one with the unity of the Father, the Son, and the Holy Spirit" (C 4:3). It is a family united under the bishop (L 26:1); its task is to show the world the mystery of God's love for his world family (CT 45:1).

Although there are many different and complementary ways of understanding the Church, the one aspect common to them all is some dimension of union, communion, love, community—that is, of family life. A brief look at some of the Vatican Council's descriptions of the Church will highlight how each of them relates to the qualities of family.

When referred to as the messianic people, the Church is understood to be a "sure seed of unity, hope, and salvation for the whole human race" (C 9:5). When the Church is described as the bride of Christ, we are reminded of the resulting values of the union and community he sets up (C 6:5; 7:9; 39:1). Seen as institution, the Church is understood at once as a visible assembly and a spiritual community (CT 40:3), and the union is so profound that we are presented with the analogy of the incarnation (C 8:1). Furthermore, the Church is a sacrament, and this means it is a sign both of intimate union with God and of the unity of the whole human race (C 1:2). The Church is also the mystical body of Christ calling us to a union with both head and members.

This link of unity and community with every feature of the Church is a trend seen throughout the documents of Vatican II. One document puts it simply: "The promotion of unity belongs to the innermost nature of the Church . . ." (CT 42:3). This call and challenge is also seen throughout Jesus' life. He preached the arrival of the kingdom of God, and as the initial flowering of this, we have the post-Easter phenomenon of the Church (C 5:4), a people, a community, a family, in which Jesus sets individuals in a new relationship to one another because of their new relationship to himself. Moreover, our relationship to Jesus is established in the Spirit so that the Easter mystery gives birth to a new creation, the Church, that is made up of all those who have the Spirit as their life. Jesus did not rise alone but rose as the firstborn of the community of people consecrated to him.

When we refer to this new group life that developed after the resurrection, we call it people of God, pilgrim people, chosen assembly of the Lord, household or family of the Lord, mystical body of Christ, total Christ. Always we use terms that describe its community characteristics. One description of the Church that seems to be the underpinning of much of the Council's teaching is the Augustinian presentation of the Church as one mystical person, having one life in which the community shares.

The biblical basis for this understanding of the Church as a mystical person is the Old Testament notion of corporate personality, which is ultimately a theological portrayal of the absolute conviction that the group—be it parents and children, clan, or nation—is a family. There is such an intimate identity among the members that their love, their life, their responsibility, their moral obligations, and their growth are conditioned by the family or corporate personality to which they belong. There is a total identification with the group, and their spiritual call is to develop the unity of the group.

The concept of corporate personality also pervades the New Testament. See, for example, the last judgment scene (Mt. 25) and Paul's conversion on the way to Damascus (Acts 9:4-5). In addition, the notion is presumed in all of Paul's teachings on the mystical body. All these New Testament uses derive from the conviction that the Christians are now seen as a family called to such intimate union that they can be described as one person.

This intimate union of Christians draws on the Holy Trinity as the model of its life. When we speak of the Holy Trinity, we believe in one nature, one God, but three persons. And when we speak of the incarnation of Christ, we speak of one person but two natures. So when we speak of the Church, we speak of the mystical body of Christ. This means we believe in one person present, living, acting, and loving in many people. But it is the Holy Spirit who is the one person acting in Christ, and so this corporate life in which we share is the life of the Spirit within us (see Eph. 4:4). The same Spirit is in Christ as in us, with the identical desire to work in us for our sanctification, and through us in service to others, with the identical power, limited only by our sinfulness. The Church is Christ's body through which the Holy Spirit wishes to continue to work exactly as he did through Christ.[12] Speaking of the Church, the Second Vatican Council stated: "By communicating His Spirit to His brothers, called together from all peoples, Christ made them mystically into His own body" (C 7:1). Together as Church we share one common life, and it is as if we all have the same name.

We begin this corporate life at baptism, when we enter the Church that Christ founded after his resurrection. "As the firstborn of many brethren and through the gift of His Spirit, he founded after his resurrection a new brotherly community composed of all those who receive him in faith and in love. This He did through His body, which is the Church" (CT 32:4). After baptism we are like new creatures because we no longer live by ourselves; we have the Holy Spirit in us just as Christ had the Holy Spirit in him. At baptism, receiving this influx of new life, we become parts of a new creature, the Church, which is a family, and whose life is the Holy Spirit.

The Spirit's relationship to the Church, as reflected on by the Second Vatican Council, can be summed up in the following text:

In order that we may be unceasingly renewed in Him, He has shared with us His Spirit, who, existing as one and the same being in the head and in the members, vivifies, unifies, and moves the whole body. This He does in such a way that his work could be compared by the holy Fathers with the function which the soul fulfills in the human body, whose principle of life the soul is. (C 7:8; see also Eph. 4:23; P 2:1)

The Council here describes the family of the Church by using Augustine's notion of mystical person. We must be so united that we become one person with one soul—the inner life of the Spirit. As the clan in the Old Testament was bound together by a common life shared from the one life-giving source in the generative action of the patriarch, so in the New Testament we are told "the Father is the source of life" (Jn. 5:26), and he wishes to share with us his divine nature (2 P. 1:4). In fact, "by his own choice he has generated us as his children by the message of truth" (Jm. 1:18); and "No one who has been begotten by God sins; because God's seed remains inside him" (1 Jn. 3:9).

The Church, then, is God's family. When we see all

members as one mystical person, one corporate personality, we are viewing the Church in terms of the scriptural notion of family. All of the Council's descriptions of the Church are either directly based on this notion or are based on another biblical notion (e.g., union or community) which in its turn presumes the religious concept of the corporate person. And, as I have said, the notion of corporate person is itself a theological portrayal of the Church as family. This understanding of the Church as family, with its biblical implications, is the most ascetically and spiritually demanding approach for today. It is also nontechnical enough to be appreciated by the non-theologian; it evokes appropriate attitudes among people; it deepens our understanding of Church and can help solve some of our current problems of Church structures and interrelationships.

Church Living as a Family Spirituality

The Church is a new creation, a Spirit-inspired community whose members are one corporate person, one family. The one life in which the group of believers shares must be lived out by each believer and by the group together (see Rm. 6:4; 7:6). There must be a group portrayal of this common family life-style. The early Church provides a model for our living of this demanding asceticism.

In the New Testament we witness a powerful conviction of the active presence of the Spirit in Church life. All knew that they were called together by the Spirit and in baptism sealed with his power and given his life (see 1 Co. 12:13; Rm. 8). The local community were made brothers and sisters in love through the Spirit (see Rm. 8:9,15) and kept in unity through the same Spirit (see Eph. 4:3). They were called to witness to this love and were entrusted with the Spirit's gifts for the service of the group (see 1 Co. 12). As we look back on the early Church's life, we recognize that their common belief through the Spirit is our faith; the group's memory of the Lord Jesus guided by the Spirit is tradition; and the group's written records of the Lord become, through the same Spirit, our scriptures. The same Spirit was recognized in their common prayer (see Rm. 8:26-27; 1 Co. 12:3; Ga. 4:6) and was their pledge of future resurrection (see Rm. 8:11). The life-style of the early groups of Christians is a manifestation of the Spirit-life given by Jesus to his new creation, the Church.

Even today ". . . wherever they live, all Christians are bound to show forth, by the example of their lives and by the witness of their speech, that new man which they put on at baptism, and that power of the Holy Spirit by whom they were strengthened at confirmation" (M 11:1). We in the Church still need an awareness and conviction of the oneness that is ours through our baptism and sealing in the Spirit. In turn, this sense of solidarity would help us appreciate the diversity of the Spirit's presence among us.

Unless we exist as a real family, we do not exist as Church. The Church is a large community of family communities. Family living is linked to the essence of Christianity so that the lack of family living is a lack in Christian living. To be Church demands the true love and asceticism of family. "He is not saved . . . who, though he is part of the body of the Church, does not persevere in charity. He remains indeed in the bosom of the Church, but, as it were, only in a 'bodily' manner and not 'in his heart'" (C 14:2; see M 19:2). Family must be domestic Church. Church must be family. It will be helpful now to examine the ecclesial qualities of family life and then identify the family qualities of ecclesial life.

Ecclesial qualities of family life

When the Council and the post-conciliar documents speak about family, what vision and ideal do they offer us? (We are not concerned here with the problems that face family. While these are important, it is also important to look at the vision, the hope that is ours. Neither are we concerned with an image of family in which the male has not yet outgrown the immature dominant roles of the past. We seek something that will give us reasons for living and reasons for hoping.)

The Council reminds us that men and women are social beings and can neither live nor develop fully without interpersonal relationships (see CT 12:5). Persons are basically beings in need, or rather creatures born to develop; their primary needs for companionship and their primary needs for a fuller personal development are located within the first cell, or very basis and foundation, of society, the family (CT 52:3). But this state of consecrated union, the family, is also a specific vocation in the Church; in fact, it is considered a domestic Church (see C 11:5; L 11:4; CT 48:4). Because the family is blessed by Christ in a special way (see CT 32:2; 48:4), the activities of married life are integrated into full human Christian living.

The married state is not only a specific vocation in the Church; it is also an institution (CT 47:2), a community, a covenant of love (CT 48:1), "a society in its own original right" (RF 5:1). The Council, while emphasizing that matrimony is based on an "irrevocable personal consent" that creates a sacred bond that "no longer depends on human decisions alone" (CT 48:1), underlines the fact that the fundamental nature of marriage lies in its being a covenant of love. The family group is a community of love wherein human qualities mature, and wherein men and women find a means of complete salvation and Christian holiness. Husband, wife, and children, in total solidarity, enrich one another, for together they bring into being human values otherwise unattainable. Serving one another, they bring one another closer to Christ. "The family is a kind of school of deeper humanity" (CT 52:1). Parents not only give; they also learn and receive from their children.

In serving each other and their children, married people exercise their first apostolic attitude within the family by their example. The ordinary circumstances of family life, which are the setting of this apostolate, are of unique importance for the Church (see C 31:3; L 11:1); the family is a sign to the world of the nature of the Church (see C 35:4; L 11:5). In this primary community, the primary apostolate is that of being a community. This being a community has a "very decisive bearing on . . . the personal development and eternal destiny of the individual members of a family . . ." (CT 48:2). In this way the family is in miniature the sacrament of union that the Church is called to be.

Marriage is a sacramental pledge of total self-giving; it is an irrevocable personal covenant and the sign of Christ's love for the Church (see CT 48:4). Marriage is, like Church, a great mystery, not because it is puzzling or unintelligible, but because it is so rich in meaning and can be grasped but partially, painfully, and gradually. One aspect of this rich mystery is the sharing of faith. "In such a home husband and wife find their proper vocation in being witnesses to one another and to their children of faith in Christ and love for Him" (C 35:4; see CT 48:7).

For spouses, then, the married life is a specific way of holiness (see CT 52:9) and of total human development. *Humanae Vitae* sees marriage from the integrally human point of view (art. 7) and deals expressly with the mutual perfecting of partners (art. 8). Marriage is a school of holiness (see Ed 7:2). Family love comes to involve the good of the whole person (see CT 49:2), affecting each one's personal development and eternal salvation (see CT 48:2); this family love is eventually "caught up into divine love . . . and can lead the spouses to God" (CT 48:5).

Thus family life is a life of consecration to the development of one another. There is nothing ready-made, and there are no finished products. This life is an asceticism of unity, a living of the paschal mystery. In addition to fostering the spouses' human and Christian development, the love shared by spouses also creates another image of God. "A love which resists being fruitful resents the full realization of itself."[13] It is only in its creative aspects that this love completely develops the spouses: . . . "only here does the personality of both reach the full abundance of its capacity for development."[14] This, too, is mission: It is the willing acceptance of the task of being creative cooperators with God and interpreters of his love (see CT 50:3).

An important aspect of the parents' mission is the education of their children. "Since parents have conferred life on their children, they have a most solemn obligation to educate their offspring" (Ed 3:1). Education is truly a divine attribute when it is seen either as the ability to creatively contribute to another's growth or as the development of oneself in discovering the unique individuality of another. Education, then, is a mutually enriching task (see CT 48:8) and consists not only in personal human formation (see Ed 3:1; 7:2; CT 52:2; 61:2) but also in Christian initiation into evangelical life. Seen in this way, "the whole of family life . . . would become a sort of apprenticeship for the apostolate" (L 30:2).

This apprenticeship includes fostering an awareness of being Church and developing a sense of responsibility for all aspects of the Church (see L 30:2). "Let families flourish which are penetrated by the spirit of the gospel" (M 15:4). The major gospel witness given by families is that of faithfulness and harmony (see CT 49:7; L 11:5): signs of the love that the Lord revealed to the world (CT 52:9). The family has a noble mission to show the world what true love is (CT 48-49). Through this mission, families share in the very mission of the Church.

Brief though it is, this sketch of Church teachings since the Council shows some key stages in family development and demonstrates the ecclesial qualities of family life. As we saw, family life develops interpersonal relationships and is a specific vocation in the Church. It is initiated by an irrevocable personal commitment to community, but it leads to mutual enrichment and deeper humanity. The family is also a domestic Church, the sacrament of union in miniature. It is a rich mystery that in faith leads us in some way to be ready to lose our own identity and, through an asceticism of unity, to find a fruitfulness formerly unthought of. In the education of their children, parents develop themselves in discovering the unique individuality of others. Essentially, they foster an awareness of being Church and yet are willing to withdraw humbly and prudently when the young person is prepared to lead an independent life. Often what they see then and still love is very different from what they thought they had created.

All of these qualities of family life are significant for the Church today. Since the strength of any organization lies in the strength of its primary groups, the Church's strength will be in the small groups that comprise it, and chief of these is the family. Any successful image or model, then, must be one rooted in the experience of the family and of other primary groups.

Family qualities of ecclesial life

While integral qualities of family life are identifiable as essential ecclesial qualities, it is also clear that ecclesial life requires much that is based in the family. The specific attitudes and qualities necessary for good healthy ecclesial life are also the attitudes and qualities necessary in the daily situations of a layperson's involvement in civil society's and the Church's primary groups. Laity are not the non-experts they have been presumed to be, but are rather the experts! This awareness that laity have much to contribute would seem more acceptable also from the perspective of faith. It is ludicrous to imply that the vast majority of those who make up the Church have next to nothing to contribute, especially when one remembers that the Church is a corporate person.

The Church is a family. To be Church, to live as Church, means to live as a part of this family, aware that we need others. No one is complete in isolation, and no member can be left out. What is true of the layperson's family is true of the Church as well. There must be unity and respect for all members, a mutual appreciation among all, and a freedom for the adults of the group. While we acknowledge the need for growth in independence, we must also reject establishing private "kingdoms" that destroy the sharing of the group. In each person there must be an irrevocable personal commitment to the group, and all must contribute actively to its life, since each one has a task to fulfill.[15]

We can only be Church today and be relevant to the world in which we live when we tap and develop the rich variety of people's gifts from the Spirit. Just as parents must tap and develop the potentials of their children, so too must all in the Church discover and parent the unique individuality of each of the baptized. In building Christ's family, every baptized person has a part to play (C 7; 32).

At times we are concerned about others' involvement in Church life: about such things as their religious education, background, skills, and style of service. However, just as we love all members of our family, so we are called to love all members of our Church, whatever their contribution, since we all share the same Spirit and life (C 12). Just as parents are proud of their children's talents, so Church leaders must delight in the gifts of all the baptized. In addition, our involvement in Church life means that eventually we, like parents, must be willing to let other Christians lead their own lives as they become adult in faith; we might then see and still appreciate something possibly very different from what we thought we had created.

An important aspect of recognizing the gifts of others lies in leading them to recognize and use their gifts themselves. For example, parents might possibly always do things themselves if they wanted work done in the most efficient way. But for families it is important to do things together in order that a sense of community may grow and so that all members may recognize their unique contribution to the group. This working together builds up family life more than efficiency does. In Church life, too, it is less important to get things done than it is to get things done in union with others and thus portray the unity for which Christ prayed. In both family and Church we grow individually by growing together. The document on the *Church* says this well: "Through the common sharing of gifts and through the common effort to attain fullness in unity, the whole and each of the parts receives increase" (C 13:3). The sharing of the family's gifts among its members develops the quality of the family's life, but this sharing is for the good of the whole Church. It was for this reason that Christ gifted his baptized (C 18).

He continually distributes in His body, that is, in the Church, gifts of ministries in which, by His own power, we serve each other unto salvation so that, carrying out the truth in love, we might through all things grow up into Him who is our head. (C 7:7)

Nowadays we recognize that the development of family life is the responsibility of all members, and this is likewise the case for the Church (C 33). In ecclesial life this co-responsibility is required, not for efficiency or democracy, but because of faith. Our faith in the Church needs to be expressed in all the members of this family working together (CT 76:3; C 35). It is time for the courageous involvement of all people in the Church, together as one family.

Just as individuals in a family cannot be family on their own, neither can the Church's members accomplish its mission in isolation or singlehandedly (P 7:6); it is intervocational ministry that portrays the nature of the Church (L 18:1). The dialogue and cooperation that this demands is itself growth-producing and is essential both for healthy family life and for healthy Church life.

In addition, the mission of all Christians is to live as the family of the Church. It is more important to *be* Church than to *do* anything. If we as Church are the family of God and are called to live as such, then it seems that the spirituality of the whole Church depends on the spirituality of small family groups within the Church. For married persons this will be their own family; for single persons, their family or friends; for religious, their community; for diocesan priests, the presbyterate. The intensity and depth of the family spirituality of the Church as a whole depends in large part on the richness of these smaller groups, and each should enrich the other. It must always be remembered that all the baptized are called to build, and that all are gifted to build.

Laity as Integrally Church

In *The Gulag Archipelago,* the Russian writer Solzhenitsyn exclaimed: "I had begun to sense a truth inside myself: if in order to live it is necessary not to live, then what's it all for?"[16] These are the sentiments of many laity today who, despite their increased education, faith development, and commitment, find themselves still confined to a passive role in the Church. Many laity have dedicated their lives to Christ as truly as have priests and religious, and they wish to live out that dedication. Other laypersons are still at the crossroads of active or passive commitment and need to be drawn to an awareness of the extensive challenges of baptism. One author, calling for a "new direction" in the Church's approach to laity, suggests: "It will be realized only if the 'non-clergy' are willing to move up, if the 'clergy' are willing to move over, and if all God's people are willing to move out."[17]

The laity's increased involvement in the life of the Church in recent years is not due to any desire to supplant the cleric. In fact, the laity's awareness of their responsibilities is largely the result of the pastoral leadership and formation work of visionary clerics and religious. Rather, it is an evangelical contestation motivated by faith and love. Laity wish to see their life and role evaluated more positively. They are, after all, the foundational Church and need to be acknowledged as an integral part of ecclesial life.

Theological evaluation of the life and role of laity

Chapter 1 identified some recent historical developments in our understanding of the life and role of laity. Most people today who are interested in redefining the specifics of lay life do so unencumbered by the inadequate theologies of recent centuries; they start by evaluating the present life and role of laity as Church and confront this current synthesis with the biblical vision of life in the early Church.[18] This approach avoids giving theological significance to historical relationships, such as the subordinate role of laity in general and of women in particular, that are primarily social and educational and of little or no theological importance. Confronting the synthesis of the life and role of laity with the biblical vision becomes a corrective against positions that are presumed and lived today but that are not theologically well based.

Four features of our Church life today determine our understanding of the life and role of laity.

First is the lived experience of the Vatican Council's insight that the Church is a community. This awareness that as Church we are primarily a mystery of community has two important implications: We are all co-responsible for the life, organization, and mission of the community; and we are all called to holiness. These two implications precede any structuring—hierarchical or vocational—of the Church.[19] This means that all of us—not just the hierarchy—are called to be co-responsible for the Church; there is no room for a passive laity. And it means that all of us—not just religious—are called to holiness; the laity are not meant to live on some subordinate level of commitment.

The second feature is the incarnational emphasis of Christian life and spirituality.[20] This awareness, developed since the turn of the century, was embodied in the Council's definition of the Church as sacrament of the world. It implies that we see the essence of the Church, not in terms of its internal structure, but in terms of its being a sacramental presence in ever-changing world conditions.[21] The usual way of living as Church is lay life, and the clerical and religious vocations are exceptions which, though they are important and enrich the Church, can in no way be the pattern for lay spirituality.

The third characteristic of today's Church that helps us understand the life and role of laity is the post-conciliar emphasis on ministry. Lay involvement is not simply a fad; it is of the essence of Christian life and is here to stay. We need to recognize both the daily reality of lay ministry and its theological implications.[22] Some members minister to the ecclesial community's own internal needs, and this is important even though secondary. However, all the baptized, by the very fact of their baptism, minister in Christ's name to the whole world, which he came to save. This rediscovery of the universal call to ministry is certainly a component of our understanding of lay life today.[23]

The fourth feature that clarifies the life and role of laity is this decade's emphasis on Christianity's need to be committed to liberation at all levels of life and society. This redemptive thrust of today's Church focuses on the transformational involvement of laity.

The importance of all the baptized was not fully appreciated until the Church rediscovered in our time these four features: (1) that we are all community (2) called to reincarnate the Lord's message (3) through our shared ministry, (4) which leads to the liberation of the world. These are the tasks of the whole Church. In fact, as Chapter 1 pointed out, there are really no distinguishing characteristics of lay life outside the general challenge to live as Church; rather there are only specifics of clerical and religious life that lead us to speak of a spirituality of the cleric or religious. Laity are Church, with the responsibilities of all the baptized. The conciliar documents moved from a negative and clerical definition of laity in 1962 to the Christological and ecclesial vision of the layperson in the documents of 1964.[24] These developments have been further complemented with the insights of the years since Vatican II.

We do not aim to devalue clerical service, nor do we wish to see the laity's service as a stopgap measure where there is a shortage of clergy. Rather, the four characteristics just discussed reemphasize the unity of the whole people of God in life, call, ministry, and prophetical challenge.

Laity as foundational Church

We have previously considered the interrelationship

between the Church as family and the family as domestic Church. The notion of family is applicable to many forms of primary groups within the Church: husband, wife, and children; husband and wife; single-parent families; divorced; single men and women. We have also seen that it is used to describe both diocesan and religious-life structures. The basic cell of Church, whatever form it takes, can be referred to as a family, and yet this term most frequently refers to primary lay groups.

These small cells of ecclesial life have been called the foundational Church.[25] This Church in miniature, basic cell and domestic Church, "constitutes the Church in its essential dimension,"[26] as John Paul II has pointed out.

If ecclesial life is not strong in the primary group cells of lay life, it cannot be strong at any other level. What is presumed in this understanding of foundational Church is "a view of the Church from below, where component communities of the wider Church are seen as establishing the foundation for the Church's life."[27] Whatever is built on this foundation will be strong or weak in proportion to the strength or weakness of this foundation.

While there are many examples of foundational Church in small lay groups, one most commonly mentioned in Church documents is the traditional family of married couple and children. The present chapter directs our attention to this domestic Church, and the conclusions will be significant regarding the earlier section of the chapter on "Church as Family." However, the conclusions will be equally valuable for the many other forms of ecclesial family life, even though those forms will need to be adapted.

The Vatican Council stated explicitly that "the Christian family . . . will manifest to all men . . . the genuine nature of the Church" (CT 48:8). Throughout salvation history, family life has always been used as the natural prime image of the deepest religious values. Idolatry and sin were described as prostitution (see Jer. 3:1; Ho. 1:2; Rev. 2:14-23), and when Yahweh threatens to withdraw his care, he says the result will be like the absence of the joys of married life (see Jer. 16:1-4).

God's attitudes to his people are described in the imagery of marriage and family (see Song of Songs, Hosea, Ezk. 16:1-14), and Jeremiah goes so far as to portray God's conquering grace in sexual terms (see Jer. 20:7). The New Testament speaks frequently of family values, wedding feasts, marital love, union, and covenant. In fact, the relationship of Christ and his Church is a marriage (see Eph. 5:21-33; Rev. 22:17; C 1:2).

Previously we saw that essential values of family life are also essential values of Church life. Seeing Church as family gives us an understanding that is immediately familiar to laity. The foundational Church of family is also a context where crucial Christian concepts can best be understood. Mystery, faithfulness, love, and union are the fabric of both marriage and Christian commitment. The tension between fear and hope or love and hate or self-gift and exploitation is something with which the married person can identify. Images of passionate search, seduction, and physical ecstasy are frequently used by religious writers and mystics to describe even the profoundest religious values. There is a natural and foundational interrelationship between family and Church in their essence and in their prime values. Church happens at the level of the family; if it does not develop there, then its presence at any other level of the Church, though possible, is always exceptional.

What are these aspects of Church developed at the family level? Within family life the parents are co-creators and cooperators with God (L 11). Before all other aspects of the ecclesial community, the family must be a school of holiness (see C 35; CT 48), of social virtues (see Ed 3), of ministry (see C 35), and of the social defense of family values (see CT 52). Evangelization starts in the basic ecclesial cell of family, which is both the prime object of evangelization and the "fundamental subject of evangelization." "Family catechesis precedes, accompanies and enriches all other forms of catechesis."[29] This is not to be understood in a chronological sense to mean that children are given rudimentary introduction to faith in the family before they go to school.

Thomas comments:

> The family is clearly the foundational community of
> the Church which also means that once the foundation
> is established, it cannot be removed. The foundation
> status of the family is on-going, ordinary and
> essential.[30]

Family, the basic cell of lay life, is also the basic cell of
Church, and pastoral leaders must be more convinced of
this and direct their attention to the domestic Church. If
leaders of the official Church continue to turn a deaf ear to
laity as foundational Church, the laity will in their turn
continue to turn a deaf ear to the official Church.[31]

The Church has generally presumed that the celibate
career ecclesiastic is the best person to understand the
nature of the Church and to teach its values to others. But
when the Church is understood as the family of the Lord,
then both its essence and its values are best appreciated by
members of the foundational Church.

Laity and the Church's mission

Throughout salvation history God establishes his covenants
with the people, not just with their leaders (see Ex. 19:4-7; 1
P. 2:9-10; Heb. 9). All the people are "a chosen race, a royal
priesthood, a consecrated nation, a people set apart . . . the
People of God" (1 P. 2:9-10). It was Christ's plan to gather
together into some organized form all who would believe in
him (see C 2:2; 9:1). The conditions were possession of the
Spirit of Christ and acceptance of the ecclesial system and
the Church's means of salvation, as well as its visible structure (see C 14:2); the people were to manifest externally, by
baptism, their union with Christ and his whole family.
Baptism itself indicated entrance into the Church; and the
putting on of the new baptismal garment—reminding us of
Roman usage, where the tunic was a sign of coming of age—
was an exterior sign of full dignity and rights in the public
life of the Church. This family belonging was strikingly

portrayed by the final part of the initiation, the sharing of the family table and the breaking of bread together. This new community is the focal point of the new covenant (see CT 32:1; C 2:2; 9:1), and before all else it is to be a sign to the world of unity (see C 9:6; CT 45:1; E 2).

The essential gifts and functions of Church life belong to every baptized member. Each one is filled with the Holy Spirit and enlivened with God's gifts of faith, hope, and charity. Within the Church there is a secondary vocational distinction but a primary and essential equality. After twenty-nine sections of the document on the *Church*, the Council states: "Everything which has been said so far concerning the People of God applies equally to the laity, religious, and clergy" (C 30:1). All are endowed with charisms for the upbuilding of the Church (see C 30:2; L 3:3), and all share in the threefold office of Christ: priestly, prophetical, and royal (see L 2:2; C 10-13 and 34-36). Among all the people of God there is a true equality (see C 30:1; 32:2), a genuine freedom (see C 37:1), a profound dignity (see C 37:3), a global responsibility (see 30:2; 33:2), a sense of vocation (see C 31), and a personal union with Christ and his mission. In fact, each one has a "proper and indispensable role in the mission of the Church" (L 1:1).

The layperson has an essential part in the mission of the Church. This "derives from his Christian vocation, and the Church can never be without it" (L 1:1). Where lay involvement is lacking, "the apostolate of the pastors is generally unable to achieve its full effectiveness" (L 10:1). In fact, one document explicitly states that where lay responsibility is absent the Church is incomplete (M 21). In the Council, the Church appealed for laity to contribute with all their force to the development of the Church (see C 33) and said that this responsibility weighed heavily on laity. The Church also encouraged laity to choose new enterprises to better the Church, to cooperate in its expansion, and to develop a sense of responsibility for it (see CT 43:4; M 36).

Laity are integrally Church. Each one is "a witness and a living instrument of the mission of the Church herself"

(L 33:2). Each baptized person has both the right and the responsibility to cooperate in the Church's mission to the world, as well as the right and responsibility to contribute to the inner life and organization of the ecclesial community (see L 3:3; 16:3).

Laity's mission to the world includes evangelizing (see C 31; 35; L 6:1-3), performing charitable activities (see CT 21:6), bringing a Christian spirit to world developments (see L 7:2), enriching family life (see L 11:1; M 21:4), and facilitating social change and progress (see CT 4; 23; 26; 60; 63-64; 75; L 13:1).

Laypersons' contributions to the inner life of the Church are also affirmed (see L 10:1; C 33:4) and include liturgical participation (see L 11), community building (M 19), and co-responsibility (see L 10:2; CT 43:7; C 32:4). This last task includes offering their special competencies to the Church in the areas of administration of the Church's material goods, catechetical instruction, direction of converts, and participation in the various pastoral commissions and parochial and diocesan councils (see L 10; 17; 26; B 27; 30).

Laity are people with whom the covenant is made; they share the essential life and gifts of the Lord; they participate essentially in his mission to the world. Laity are not defined exclusively by their secular condition, as has been frequently suggested, for that condition is everyone's, including the priest and religious who live their vocations in the same context as the layperson, in interaction with the world. Nor is their life or their role determined by the temporal tasks in which they are involved, since no one's life is defined by what he or she does. Rather we can say with the Council:

> These faithful are by baptism made one body with Christ and are established among the People of God. They are in their own way made sharers in the priestly, prophetic, and kingly functions of Christ. They carry out their own part in the mission of the whole Christian people with respect to the Church and the world. (C 31:1)

It is this ecclesial characteristic that is the determinative component in the life of laity. They are integrally Church.

Conclusion

In this chapter we have identified some general lines of
consensus regarding an understanding of the Church
which is immediately familiar to laity, which portrays sufficiently the life and mission of laity, and which integrates the
role of laity within the whole life of the Church. We focused
on the concept of Church as family as being an approach
clear enough to be appreciated by all, yet symbolic enough
to evoke attitudes, relationships, and courses of action; it is a
concept that is also clear enough in its currently evolved
sociological understanding to help even in a theoretical
understanding of the Church. We also saw that it is an
approach that has potential for successfully developing
Church life in the last decades of the twentieth century.
Dulles had suggested that "one's vision of the Church
should be neither so exalted as to be out of touch with daily
experience, nor yet so empirical as to contain no mandate
for action."[32] He later regretted the Catholic Church's
inability to capitalize on the spiritual experiences of so many
faithful, and he concluded that much of the ineffectiveness
of the Church was due to the fact that many faithful just
cannot see where they fit in.[33]

In looking at the Church as family, we have seen that
there is a dynamic interrelationship between family life and
Church. There are many ecclesial qualities in everyday family life, and the layperson should know that Christian family
living is a basic training in being Church. Moreover, there
are many family qualities in ecclesial life, and the whole
Church has much to learn from the daily family experiences
of the faithful.

Laity are an intimate part of the community of the
Church: They are the point where the Christian message is
incarnated in today's societies; their ministry is the mission
of the Church; and they must bring Christ's liberating
redemption to the world. Small lay groups or basic ecclesial

cells embody the Church's life and message. Families are foundational Church; all else is built on this foundation.

Family and *Church* are both evolving notions. Relationships in family are different from what they used to be. In healthy family life there is simple structure, and parents always have a primacy of honor. Parents' roles change as their children grow up: Parents are the source of life; at one time they are authority figures; later they are friends and counselors, and sometimes even dependents. Children grow into rights of their own: They earn freedom, respect, and authority; they develop lives, visions, and hopes of their own.

Within the family of the Church there must be a real sense of community and a deep appreciation of one another. As the faithful grow, all must strive to facilitate the development of gifts in one another. There must always be real listening, sincere dialogue, and mutual obedience. Whatever roles evolve, there should be mutual support in ministry.[34]

Catholic ecclesiology has generally been descending, both in that its teachings are deduced from revealed principles and in its hierarchical structures.[35] But this present emphasis on family implies that there is also an ascending component to a Catholic ecclesiology.[36] Laity have much to contribute to Church life, for Church is constituted by the Lord on values by which the laity live each day. The Church is a community of communities, a family of families.

4

Spirituality of All the Baptized

Introduction

This has been a century of great interest in spirituality. Significant developments can be traced to the end of its first decade.[1] Vatican II stands out among all the ecumenical councils as the great council for spirituality, and papal, synodal, and episcopal documents around the time of the Council and since then have been especially significant in their spiritual challenges.[2] This move to explicit challenges in spirituality is a significant development on the part of the Church of this century in contrast with previous centuries, when Church documents principally emphasized doctrine, order, and discipline.

In addition to Church leaders' emphasizing spirituality in their teachings, a genuine commitment to Christian growth has contributed strongly to the satisfaction today of people's hopes and aspirations for personal fulfillment, social enrichment, and world development; for peace, leisure, and stable values; for personal prayer and community worship and faith; for a sense of commitment and integrated living. Moreover, as Christians face many new practical problems, they make new applications of basic evangelical challenges, and new areas of spirituality are developed.

While these observations are true and very encouraging, there is still enough misunderstanding of spirituality to cause concern. Although in faith we know that spirituality is our dynamic and efficacious incarnation of Christ's message, it is unfortunately not always appreciated in this way, and we have rarely seen a spirituality of all the baptized. To many, spirituality seems irrelevant, wishy-washy, and escapist; it seems to have little appeal and value for daily life. For many, spirituality sounds like a fad and suggests anemic or selfish images.[3]

Many reactions to spirituality today, particularly from laity, can challenge us to re-present the basic call of Jesus and emphasize a spirituality of all the baptized that integrates the profound and intimate values of life. Spirituality needs to be presented as ecclesially and universally necessary rather than as the reserve of one small group—a kind of spiritual colonialism where one spiritual movement or another sets up outposts of empire. It must be presented as the God-given way for all to the best fulfillment of human life and the way to "a greater share in existence."[4]

Clear, theologically accurate, and reasonably complete definitions of spirituality are difficult to find.[5] A simple description that highlights some key common elements was presented in a recent book on spiritual direction: "Spirituality is the style of a person's response to Christ before the challenge of everyday life, in a given historical and cultural environment."[6] Complementing this definition and enlarging on the specifics of "a person's response to Christ," Albert-Marie Besnard suggests the following:

> Spirituality refers to a living synthesis of human and evangelical elements. On the one hand spirituality is really the structuring of an adult personality in faith according to one's proper genius, vocation and charismatic gifts; and on the other hand according to the laws of the universal Christian mystery.[7]

In looking for a spirituality of all the baptized that will satisfy these requirements, we will review recent trends in spiritual development, common characteristics of Christian life, and accepted priorities in spirituality today. However, we must also be aware that the notion of spirituality evolves and changes as individuals and their historical and cultural environments change; but more importantly, that each component of spirituality changes. Our notions of God, Church, prayer, commitment, faith, sin, and so on, are constantly developing under the influences of the theological and human sciences, and as they do, so does the general concept of spirituality. There is always tension between what spirituality was in a previous generation and what it needs to be today and tomorrow.

Our generation is no exception. Spirituality for today is taking a new and different shape, even as the struggle between generations continues. We have seen that major Church documents and conferences have given a new emphasis to spirituality. In addition, people throughout the world are finding satisfaction and fulfillment in spiritual renewal. Recent trends have highlighted the common, non-elitist, and lay elements in Christian commitment, as well as the developing, changing aspects based on environment, history, culture, and individual situations. We see in present trends a convergence of values that are important to all the baptized, especially to those previously referred to as laity. This convergence of values has become the catalyst in the formation of a spirituality of all the baptized. A brief look at the history of Christian spirituality will trace the course of today's spirituality and locate its roots, from the time of Jesus on, as well as the factors, both present and past, that have influenced it.

A Brief History of Christian Spirituality

Jesus preached to men and women of all walks of life and successfully challenged good people and sinners; sick and healthy; respected women and prostitutes; simple people, civic officials, and religious leaders; fishermen, tax collectors, and centurions; Jews and Gentiles; even Zealots and Pharisees.

Although Jesus' audience included all types of people, an audience selection is already in evidence by the time the evangelists compose his life and ministry. The Marcan Jesus gives his message to all in the period preceding Peter's major expression of faith in Jesus as Messiah (8:27-30), but afterwards he directs his teachings mostly to the Twelve. In

Matthew's gospel the disciples are equated with the Twelve. Luke alone of the Synoptic writers understands disciples as *all* who come to faith in Jesus. In doing this, he complements Paul, who had also avoided restricting the notion of discipleship.

In fact, the post-resurrection Church as described in Paul and Acts shows a clear appreciation of the life and spirituality of all believers, irrespective of their roles.[8] Mark, and in a particular way Matthew, faced clearly identified local community needs and saw this literary restricting of the notion of discipleship to the Twelve as part of a response to these needs. Neither evangelist's presentation, however, could be seen as the first stage in a sanctuary spirituality.

In the scriptural descriptions of the development of the early Church, we meet many people whom we generally consider to be priests, but this identity is not stated, and several were probably not priests. However, there is a host of dedicated and actively committed members of the early Church who most certainly were laypeople. There were the families of Aristobulus and Narcissus and particularly Stephanas's family, who, Paul says, "have really worked hard" to help the growth of the early Church (1 Co. 16:15). There were the dedicated married couples Aquila and Priscilla, fellow workers of Paul (Rm. 16:3-4; Ac. 18:2; 1 Co. 16:19), Tryphaena and Tryphosa, "who work hard for the Lord" (Rm. 16:12). Then there were Rufus and his mother, Nereus and his sister, Hermas and her brothers, and Nympha, who organized the Church in her home (Col. 4:15). To these families we can add a host of individuals—men and women who were a vital part of the life and growth of the early Church: Andronicus and Junias, "those outstanding apostles" (Rm. 16:7), Ampliatus, Hermes, Epaenetus, Urban and Cornelius. There were also Mary, dedicated to the Roman Church, and Dorcas, a disciple "who never tired of doing good" (Ac. 9:36). In original Christianity, then, the challenge of the call of discipleship was for all the people.[9] Today's vocational distinctions in spirituality would have been out of place in New Testament times.[10]

Early developments

The preaching of the apostles as we find it in their writings always treated the values of lay life with respect, reverence, and a positive appreciation of how a Christian approach to community, money, sex, and marriage led to God. There was no suggestion of a rejection of these aspects of life except in Paul's writings when he still believes the return of the Lord is imminent. In general, both Paul and Peter speak positively of the integration of these values into a God-directed life—values that are still considered to be the specifics of a lay condition: community qualities (see Rm. 12:1-13; 1 Th. 5:12-22), political and civic life (Rm. 13:1-7; 1 P. 2:13-17), marriage and sexual morality (1 Co. 6:5—7:40; Eph. 5:21-33; Col. 3:18-25; 1 P. 3:1-7), financial affairs (2 Co. 8 and 9). In addition, it must be recalled that all the New Testament writings, with but a few exceptions (e.g., parts of the letters to Titus and Timothy), are directed to an audience that has no vocational distinctions within it.

After the death of the apostles, the Fathers of the Church continued to preach this universal call to holiness and this positive appreciation of the constitutive elements of the life of all the baptized.[11]

But there were three trends in these early centuries that negatively influenced the development of a spirituality of all the baptized: dualistic philosophies and heresies; the development of monasticism; and the consolidation of the institutional dimensions and the development of the clerical dimensions of the Church. Obviously, each of these trends contributes to important positive growth for the Church, but a side effect in each case was a discrediting and disdaining of the life of the average baptized person.

One of the first heresies that the Church reacted against was the Encratic heresy, which was an attack on the sexual life of the married. This attack was already found in apocryphal writings of the second century. During the second and third centuries, several dualistic heresies considered matter as evil: Gnosticism (taught in Rome by Valentinus around 140), Montanism (c. 150), and Manichaeism (in

Palestine and Asia Minor around 274). This dualism, with its negative approach to the material aspects of daily life, surfaced also in Neo-Platonism (Plotinus, 203-279). Although the Church condemned the heresies, a negative approach to matter remained, and an exaggerated spiritualism developed, particularly in Fathers of the Church who were especially influenced by Neo-Platonism (Origen, Basil, Gregory of Nyssa, Augustine). Disdain and scorn for normal, everyday material life, as well as a glorification of "flight from the world" constantly resurfaced in Christianity throughout all subsequent centuries up to and into the twentieth.

A second trend that negatively influenced the development of a spirituality for all the baptized was the development of monasticism. In the early Church the perfection of one's commitment to the Lord was attained in martyrdom. The martyr was the saint and model of holiness. With the passing of the persecutions, the death of the body was spiritualized and applied first to virginity and later more broadly to the whole life of the ascetic, whose penances and abstinence were seen as a sacrifice of one's life for Christ. Those who wished to give themselves fully to Christ would first choose to be martyrs; or if that were not possible, they would accept the monastic life with its emphasis on virginity and flight from the world. Already in the second century there were ascetics in the near East and northern Africa, while in the early third century there were a few ascetics in the West. By the mid-third century the ascetic's life included withdrawal from society, and by the fourth century the first structured forms of cenobitism (a form of monasticism that was partly community and partly hermit life) emerged, followed later by full community life.

During the persecutions all the baptized were exposed to martyrdom, but with the development of monasticism came the first idea of a state of perfection, the first tiered approach to Christian spirituality, and the first signs of a "second-class-citizen" attitude toward the general body of the baptized.[12] By the fourth century there was also a spiritual elite, seen as teachers and offering a diluted form of their monastic spirituality to all the baptized.

The third trend that affected lay spirituality negatively—the consolidation of the institutional aspects of the Church and the development of a clerical group—was already identifiable in Ignatius of Antioch (d. 107), and even in Clement of Rome (c. 96). What concerns us in this third trend is not the doctrinal issues but rather the negative impact on the spirituality of all the baptized that resulted from this early sharp distinction between leaders and followers; from the early equation of charism and office; from the identification of the mission of Jesus with the ministry of the hierarchy; and from the sacralization of office.[13] Even if these developments are considered to be of divine institution, the resulting diminished role of all the baptized was nevertheless at least pastorally shocking.[14]

Already in the early centuries, then, the emphases in spirituality were elitist, and the models and means were extraordinary. There was a clearly identified move away from the values of the ordinary Christian and a rejection in practice of the spiritual value of those issues that make up lay life.

Monasticism's magnetism

By the time of Gregory the Great (d. 604), the laity were mere "children of the Church," and the clergy were "shepherds, preachers, teachers, rulers, prelates."[15] In the gospels, preaching of the evangelical call had been directed to everyone, but a chasm had already formed in the universal audience that Jesus had addressed. According to writers and preachers of the time, there were now the rulers of the people, sent like the prophet Balaam to guide, and there were the children, who were stubborn like Balaam's ass. There were the ascetic contemplatives, beautiful like Jacob's second wife Rachel, and there were the hard-working Christians, a little blear-eyed like Leah.[16] In comparisons such as these, the average baptized Christian of the time did not fare well!

At the same time that these distinctions were being drawn, monastic spirituality acted like a magnet, drawing to its imitation all who wished to be committed to Christ. It was as if baptism were no longer enough. Although Jesus' basic attitude toward world values was optimistic, monastic spirituality from the start despised the world and "died to the world" in an imitation of the martyrdom of the early Church. Moreover, this attitude was seen as the key practical component of a faithful love of the Lord. Laity's piety mirrored this view: Many abandoned civil society to enter the monastery, and others at least took up residence close to the monastery, where they could live a partial monastic penance. This latter group were seen as the lay elite of their day, but their life and spirituality were monastic, not lay.

The reign of Charlemagne (768-814) and the reforms of Pope Gregory VII (1073-1085) are notable for their contributions to lay spirituality.[17] During Charlemagne's reign the usual lay audience of leaders, princes, and lawyers was enlarged to include married people. But the systematic spirituality that resulted from Charlemagne's reforms was still an application of monastic practices. The Gregorian reforms affected lay spirituality in two outstanding ways. First, teachings for laity moved from spirituality to morality: from Jesus' call to his commands, from spiritual growth to the avoidance of sin. This minimalistic approach hampered the Church right up to the new integration of these two theological disciplines undertaken by Bernard Häring in the 1960s. Second, the Gregorian reforms separated the ecclesiastical and secular spheres, assigning the former to clerics and the latter to laity.

Monasticism's magnetic influence over spirituality continued in the eleventh century. Benedictines began to admit lay brothers; crusading lay knights began to come together in quasi-religious orders like the Knights Templar; and diocesan clergy began to assemble into orders of Canons Regular. In each case we see monastic spirituality applied to other vocations for which it was and still is unsuitable.

Elements of monasticism—community life, the breviary, celibacy, obedience—were then imposed on non-monastic clergy. Certain elements of monasticism were also imposed on laity: forms of prayer, styles of penance, negative approach to matter, anti-sexual bias, and a form of obedience to their pastors that resembled the obedience of religious to their superiors.

The devotions and piety of the laity had many excellent qualities. Devotions to the Word of God as found in scripture, to Jesus (especially in the Blessed Sacrament) and to Mary flourished in the twelfth and thirteenth centuries. True "conversion," however, was still identified with entrance into religious life, and the quality of spiritual commitment was measured in proportion to one's withdrawal from everyday life and entrance into a monastic environment. One writing of the day, reflecting this tiered concept, refers to "wife, widow and virgin" and assures them respectively of thirty, sixty, and a hundredfold reward.[18] A similar issue was debated by Thomas Aquinas (1225-1274) and some of his opponents. Thomas's thesis was that religious life was a state of perfection; his opponents argued that the priesthood was a state of perfection. While both sides appreciated the significance of baptismal commitment, it is significant that the contest was between religious life and the priesthood. Such an attitude has clearly hindered the development of a spirituality of all the baptized.

The fourteenth and fifteenth centuries witnessed the growth of lay guilds, confraternities, and some forms of temporary common life. The vernacular, increasingly used in writings, made those writings more accessible to laity. Some movements encouraged strong lay involvement, and these two centuries also saw such outstanding lay saints as St. Frances of Rome, St. Catherine of Siena, and St. Nicholas of Flüe.[19] It was also at this time that an unknown author, possibly Thomas à Kempis (1380-1471), wrote the *Imitation of Christ* as an attempt to make spirituality accessible to all.

In the sixteenth and seventeenth centuries, several outstanding Christian humanists such as Thomas More (d.

1535) and Erasmus (d. 1536), both in their writings and lives, began to show a more positive valuing of the lay condition and lay spirituality. This valuing reached a special insight in the universal call to holiness in the writings of Francis of Sales (1608, *Introduction to the Devout Life*; 1616, *Treatise on the Love of God*), as we will see further in a moment.

After New Testament times, the history of spirituality up to the time of Francis of Sales is basically the history of the influence of monasticism. Two features of late medieval Church architecture are significant in this regard. One is the rood screen. It eventually became a complete wall separating the laity from the liturgy, which was celebrated in the sanctuary by the clergy. The other is the convent cloister and grille, which in practice kept the laity out. The rood screen, cloister, and grille typified ecclesiastical attitudes toward the "ordinary" Christian.

Later developments

In the period following the reform of 1500-1650, there were large-scale efforts at renewal of faith and at religious and spiritual commitment. Spirituality was now more accessible to all; it was practical and more closely related to daily life. A strong individual and personal dimension surfaced in an emphasis on personal mental prayer.

Although the most visible spiritual developments were among the great Spanish and Italian mystics from religious orders, the emphases on personal, affective, popular spirituality were seeds of a more universally applicable Christian challenge. Along with the sixteenth-century rebirth of the great schools of spirituality—Benedictine, Franciscan, Augustinian, and Dominican—several new schools of spirituality appeared in Spain and France. Two Spanish schools, the Ignatian (Ignatius of Loyola, 1491-1556) and the Carmelite (Teresa of Avila, 1515-1582, and John of the Cross, 1542-1591), merit mention here since they show moderation in ascetical practices, a focus on Jesus, an integration of prayer and action, and a popular Marian piety. Both schools gave the Church clear methods of spiritual development and forms of spiritual growth that were to have broad application to the people of God.

Two great French contributors of this period were Cardinal de Bérulle (1575-1629) and Francis of Sales (1567-1622). In his development of a priestly spirituality, the former particularly influenced the clergy, but the latter must be singled out as a key figure in the renewed formulation of the universal call to holiness. His preface to the *Introduction to the Devout Life* could act as a synthesis of our glance at history so far:

> Nearly everyone who has written about the spiritual life has had in mind those who live apart from the world, or at least the devotion they advocate would lead to such retirement. My intention is to write [for] those who have to live in the world and who, according to their state, to all outward appearances have to lead an ordinary life.[20]

One commentator says that Francis achieves his purpose "in an optimistic, human, and irresistible manner."[21]

After the death of Francis, but before the end of the seventeenth century, the Church faced three periods of crisis in spirituality. These crises were provoked by Illuminism (which emphasized the absolute and autonomous value of nature and reason), Jansenism (which emphasized that the human will is always sinful in its actions), and Quietism (which emphasized union with God through passivity and denied the value of any preparation). At the time, these movements led to secularization, pessimism, and passivism, but eventually they called for an integration of the world into Christian life, for optimistic approaches in life, and for a balance of active-passive commitment.

The final movement to be mentioned in this rapid overview of those aspects of Christian history significant for lay spirituality developed first in America. When it later spread to Europe, it eventually developed into a movement called Modernism, whose doctrinal developments were condemned by Rome (1898-1907). Its original concerns in America were pastoral, and its basic principles emphasized liberty, internal inspiration by the Holy Spirit, natural virtues, and the active virtues of daily life. However, some of the pastoral and spiritual needs that nourished the roots of the movement remained unanswered in the life and spirituality of the average Christian.

The twentieth century has been a period of great spiritual revival. I have already referred to the outstanding popes of this period and their clear leadership in spiritual reform. I have also mentioned the biblical, liturgical, lay apostolic, and ecumenical movements with their life challenges. In Chapter 1, I indicated the theologians of this century who gave us a theology of matter, world, marriage, and religious liberty; I pointed out ecclesiologists and biblical and patristic scholars whose research presented new insights into our faith that are of major significance for lay spirituality. There have also been outstanding laity like Friedrich von Hügel, Frank Duff, Frank Sheed, Jacques Maritain, Dorothy Day, and Jean Vanier. Another phenomenon of this century has been the grass-roots spiritual movements that have developed in every country and have been another sign of the evangelical vitality of the Church.[22]

The culminating ecclesial experience of this century was Vatican II. This ecumenical council confronted the pastoral and spiritual needs of the generation and presented an inspiring and profoundly challenging synthesis. It did not give superficial, one-sided answers to profound problems but urged balance, integration, and a "both/and" attitude to issues that had created spiritual tension in previous generations: institution/mystery, office/charism, transcendence/humanism, obedience/co-responsibility, heavenly values/earthly values, individual/community, flight from the world/involvement, fidelity to the past/renewal, liberty/commitment, and unity/pluralism.

In the conciliar teachings, the basis of spiritual growth is the sacramental system of the Church. Christ, through the sacraments of the Church, is the source of all holiness, particularly in baptism, confirmation, and Eucharist (see C 11; 40:2). This growth is celebrated and deepened in the liturgical life in which we all share, and it is made concrete for each person by the sacraments of vocation. The real director of the spiritual life is the Holy Spirit, who in the sacraments consecrates all in the priestly, prophetical, and royal office of Christ. He gives to all the baptized the *sensus fidei* (the consensus regarding faith) and personal charisms (see C 12; 35).

The vision of the Church that emerges from the Council leads us to reaffirm a New Testament position frequently lost sight of in practice: the call of all the Church to holiness (see C 41-42; 40:1). God's call is to all the baptized, and the essence of holiness is not some extreme and unusual asceticism but charity (see C 40:3; L 8; C 41:7). All are called to the perfection of charity, called to permeate moral life, its laws and obedience with charity, to let charity draw them to the evangelical counsels (see C 42:5). The Council's teaching on holiness does not refer to distinctions, degrees, or grades. It is one and the same holiness shared by all (see C 41:1). There are a variety of charisms and a variety of vocations within the one holiness. Even the spirituality of priest (P 12) and religious (C 44:2) is seen as an intensification of their baptismal commitment.

Within the conciliar teaching it would seem more accurate, then, to speak first of a holy Church in whose holiness individuals participate (see C 39). The Church is called to be holy, and it lives out this call in the sacraments, in prayer, in fidelity to the Word, in the charisms of all, and in its various vocations. The vision is one of an ecclesial unity in the commitment to holiness rather than the divisive and tiered approaches of previous generations (see P 2:5). The Church is holy, and yet the Church is always in need of purification (see C 8:4). All the baptized are called to live out their spirituality by purifying the Church they are and by becoming the holy Church they are called to be.

Our glance at history has shown that the early Church emphasized equality in the Christian call to holiness. Then followed a monastic monopoly of the means of holiness and some signs of compulsive and consumeristic strivings for perfection that led to the "haves" and "have-nots" of holiness. With the post-Constantinian clericalization of the Church, ecclesiastical authorities began to "manage" spirituality. During all this time, non-lay values were emphasized, and lay values were disdained and neglected.[23] This Church-without-the-world gradually led to a world-without-Church. Vatican II reassessed these trends and opposed any exaggerated supernaturalism; it evaluated lay values positively and reaffirmed the universal call to holiness.[24]

Trends in Modern Spirituality

The second half of the twentieth century has seen notable changes in the spirituality of all the baptized. Prior to this time, spirituality was managed by the local pastor from the parish: He was the parish animator, minister of the liturgy, and, in the sacrament of reconciliation, the spiritual director of the people. Spirituality was kept alive by means of collective attitudes toward personal devotions. Spirituality was quite individualistic. One could always increase devotions by selecting from the wide range of practices offered within the parish at appropriate times of the year. The local spiritual "consumer" was offered the possiblity of security and satisfaction. Spirituality was more systematized, formal, individual, and based on accepted methods of the day.

Today, however, spirituality thrives within small support groups, and the animator and spiritual director are of personal choice. Collective attitudes are insufficient to keep the commitment alive. One must manage one's own spiritual life and live out a personal daily commitment to the communal spiritual growth of the Church. The previous parish-based unanimity has given way to many incarnations of the Christian call. Spirituality is now less systematized and more vital; there is less emphasis on formal participation and more on personal authenticity; spirituality is less individual and more communitarian; it is based less on accepted methods and more on personal spontaneity; it is less concerned with exclusively local problems and more directed to a global vision. Today there is little security to be found, for spirituality generally involves risk. In our future-shock society the problems that require a spiritual response or challenge are ever changing, and the resulting attempts to integrate Christian values and life are always new.

Several authors have addressed this issue of current trends and characteristics in the last decade. Ancilli, a professor in Rome, suggests the following trends as characterizing our age: a sense of community, a longing for the absolute, a return to sources, and an opening and commitment to the world.[25] R. Kevin Seasoltz, analyzing contemporary American lay movements in spirituality, arrives at six areas that he sees as the most helpful and characteristic of lay spirituality: It should be Christocentric, ecclesial, liturgical, both individual and communal, contemplative and ministerial, and it should have hope in the future.[26] One of the most recent analyses was made by George Aschenbrenner, who detailed fourteen trends affecting everyone in spirituality today and then added others for specific vocations.[27] The most thorough review of trends can be found in the "Current Trends" section of *Spirituality Today.*[28]

As one reviews the developments identifiable today, it seems that there are four major groupings of trends, or four major thrusts, in spirituality. First, spirituality today is *ecclesial.* This thrust includes all those trends that emphasize a sense of Church, community awareness, prayer and life of the people of God, and attitudes or styles of living that portray the group dimension of the Church. Second, spirituality today is *incarnational.* This thrust includes contemporary movements and trends that imply a positive appreciation of the world, that call for dialogue between Church and organizations and between corporate structures and science, and that lead to an integration of the spiritual and the temporal. The third major thrust is toward *service* to the world; it includes all forms of the ministry of all the baptized to the world. The fourth major thrust, which includes many trends, is itself a development of the third but has become so pronounced and extensive that it deserves specific consideration. Spirituality today is *liberational*; to be authentic it must move to liberation and justice in oneself, in others, in institutional structures—be they civil or ecclesiastical—and in the world looked at from an ecological perspective.

Ecclesial trend

In recent years we have witnessed among the baptized not only a growing awareness of what it means to be Church but also a commitment to various forms of group and community growth. Parish renewal projects such as the one sponsored by "Caritas Christi," and parish or interparish retreats such as the ones offered by the Movement for a Better World, emphasize conversion and renewal as an ecclesial experience. Some dioceses have directed their renewal efforts to setting up basic ecclesial communities.

Paralleling the parish-based renewal efforts are the spiritual movements of recent times. Laity have flooded into many of these and discovered a new spiritual call and a spirituality appropriate for them. This trend has often been called the "lay Pentecost" of our times. The most visible characteristics of the majority of these movements are sharing in faith, witness of mutual charity, and the community or ecclesial thrust of the members' lives. Even in prayer groups and charismatic groups the most visible feature is not simply prayer but the *common* prayer and praise of a believing people.

Another current trend with a strong ecclesial dimension is the movement—both organized and spontaneous—of family spirituality that we have referred to already.

All these movements have required support groups and structures to facilitate dialogue, mutual appreciation, a sense of solidarity and co-responsibility, and fidelity and perseverance in each one's commitment to the other.[29] In other words, many of today's trends, such as prayer movements and prayer groups, require group forms of asceticism or spiritual commitment. Almost all of these have added a community-ecclesial aspect to individual prayer and have reemphasized active participation in liturgies.

This community element has overflowed into a wider community awareness on a civic, national, and international level—an awareness that has led to a sense of brotherhood and sisterhood, a need to share, and a feeling of responsibility for world need. It has also led to the development of movements supporting minority rights in civil society and Church.

This first thrust in spirituality, then, is a multifaceted, willing cooperation with God, who *through Church* draws people to himself.[30] Basically ecclesial, this is a form of spiritual presence manifested in the various trends, a presence creative of Church, where the baptized invest their lives at all levels. It is a spirituality that demands the death of all forms of individualism and leads to the risen life of God's community.

Incarnational trend

The second major thrust in spirituality today is incarnational. As the previous trend reflected a new and willing cooperation with one another and with God, so this one reflects a new attitude to the world in which the Church exists. The great social encyclicals of this century prepared the way for a positive Christian encounter with world values. The life and writings of Teilhard de Chardin epitomized the Christian scientist's love for the world he studied, and they profoundly influenced future generations in their approach to the temporal. Scholars provided significant breakthroughs in Roman Catholicism's reevaluation of the world,[31] and Vatican II gave us the great *Pastoral Constitution*. These positive developments have been complemented with some healthy and purifying effects of the process of secularization, which has led to an awareness that the responsibility for removing injustices, challenging discrimination, and improving quality of life is ours and not immediately God's.

As a result of these contributions, the Church now not only sees the world positively but also envisions its own role as one of self-insertion into world realities. Christians are called to commit themselves to the temporal; to use it with detachment; to heal, animate, and transform the world; to consecrate the world to God in Christ.[32]

This positive approach to the world has led to worker-priests, secular institutes, and youth groups that emphasize social involvement; it has also opened new avenues in the understanding of Christianity's leavening presence in politics, administration, education, sexual life, and finance. A redirecting of spirituality, then, to areas of lay specialization has resulted.

Incarnational spirituality is a spirituality of influential presence. It implies a positive appreciation of the world and a self-insertion into the world to sanctify and redeem it. Of the four major thrusts I have referred to, this one has received most attention in the last fifty years. Possibly Matthew Fox and the many who have followed his spiritual lead express best the current importance of this trend. Fox speaks of a creation-centered spirituality for today instead of the fall/redemption spirituality of previous centuries.[33]

This incarnational spirituality recognizes that the world as well as its people must give glory to God, and so we have seen in recent years a greater integration of culture into liturgy; art and music have been integrated into religion and prayer; and experiences of other cultures and religions have become a greater part of Christian spiritual development. We have seen the development of professional groups—of doctors, lawyers, teachers, nurses, business people, homemakers, professors, scientists—who together strive for a greater integration of their Christian commitment and their profession.

A further trend identifiable within the incarnational

emphasis in spirituality is that of healthy appreciation of the world—an appreciation that leads, for example, to ecological concerns on a world scale and to non-possessiveness in one's own life. In addition, many of today's trends in leisure, exercise, health foods, and so on are not just fads but often have a religious basis. Today, too, our concept of "neighbor" has undergone a dramatic change as we examine our world. Some authors, reflecting on Jesus' command, suggest that "neighbor" is not just the person one meets but is also foreign cultures, nations, organizations, and so on.[34] In fact, we have come to understand that our treatment of the world is part of our very journey to God.

Service-oriented trend

The third major thrust of spirituality today is that of service to the world. Not only are we more clearly aware of who we are as Church and more fully appreciative of the world in which we live, but we see service to that world as an integral part of our spirituality. While many forms of ecclesial ministry for all the baptized have developed in recent years, the major thrust in spirituality has been for ministries to the world. Just as the incarnational thrust was an extension of the ecclesial, so this service-oriented thrust is basically a deeper commitment to the incarnational dimension.

The concept of "servant Church" is not explicitly used in the documents of Vatican II, but it certainly permeates many sections of the documents, notably numbers 40 to 44 of the *Pastoral Constitution*. Here the Church is seen as serving the world by being a leaven and soul for human society, by giving meaning and value to everyday human activity, and by having "a healing and elevating impact on the dignity of the person" (CT 40:5). The Church teaches the meaning of human existence, anchors "the dignity of human nature against all tides of opinion" (CT 41:4), proclaims the dignity of conscience and freedom of choice, advises all the baptized to use their talents for God's service and the world's, and protects human rights. On a social level the Church serves the world by insisting on family unity, by aiding the world's needy, and by being a sign and instrument of universality.

These and similar conciliar challenges have led to the development of several trends in spirituality that can be grouped under this thrust of service to the world. Sometimes we are dealing with personal life-styles; sometimes we are presented with group manifestations that are generally intervocational or lay (see L 13:1). But the basis of all these trends is the realization that all the baptized are called to see the intimate unity between their faith and the fulfillment of their daily obligations.

Many individuals, out of a sense of ministry, have committed themselves to public office in politics, finance, education, or administration. Others, often through the local diocese that has adopted a sister diocese in mission areas, volunteer for service overseas, or volunteer at home in the inner city or in poor regions of the nation. They work in health fields, education and family life, and with refugees. Others have committed themselves to a life and ministry devoted to protecting and developing human dignity in movements for human rights, in right-to-life groups, and so on. Many others are today's peacemakers in what has become for them a Christian challenge and spirituality. Others see their service to the world as best achieved by being sensitive to the world's needs and bringing these needs to the Church, and by being sensitive to the positive contribution that the world can make to the growth of the Church and bringing that contribution too (CT 44). Finally, rather than focus on personal service, many see their lives as part of the corporate calling of laity to Christianize structures of society.[35]

This thrust of service to the world can of course be referred to as the many-faceted work of evangelization—the prime ministry of us all. However, the involvement of laity in this work was stressed by the conciliar and post-conciliar documents (see C 31; 35; L 6), and it has been manifested in some of the trends I have referred to here.

Liberational trend

This fourth trend in spirituality is related to the others in that it is an intensification of or a particular aspect of serving the world, recognizing the incarnational and relational aspects of world and Church, and responding to the cry for fullness of life for this world. Since the seventies there has developed among the Christian people an acute awareness of social, structured, and cosmic sin; an appreciation that "we are all victims and all are dying from a lack of compassion";[36] and hence a concrete commitment at all levels to liberating ourselves, others, and the world from this generation's oppressions. The conviction is daily growing that spirituality is not simply individual but must be authenticated in a dedication to social justice.

In this liberational thrust of spirituality there are three key trends. The first is seen in today's emphasis on healing. On an individual, personal level this is directed against compulsiveness, competitiveness, and possessiveness, and it is turning many to a life of simplicity in which Christians deemphasize luxuries and the consumerist mentality and live in simple ways, using all superfluous wealth to help others in need. On a group level we have seen a whole spirituality of healing shared in workshops that provoke new attitudes to self and others and lead to a sharing of life with others who are no longer seen so much as "less fortunate" but as unfortunate, as we all are in our individual ways. L'Arche communities are an example of this attitude and life sharing.

The second trend is the prophetical challenge to society. This prophetical challenge—sometimes called contestation—is a personal or organized struggle against the injustices of structured society, whether civil or ecclesiastical. The former passivity of lay spirituality has hindered the development of this dimension, and we still need to educate both clergy and laity to genuine evangelical contestation. In spite of drawbacks, such as the lack of education to justice, the previous passivity of laity, and the natural reticence of some, many have become involved in social justice issues abroad and at home. Just salaries, rights of minorities, defeat of sexist positions, justice for political prisoners, opposition to unlawful governments, challenge to abuse of position, and correcting of legal injustices have all been the focus of challenge. We have also seen much organized Christian effort in the international political field through the pressures of public opinion. Others have challenged the way we all abuse the environment, and the way multinational corporations have selfishly exploited it.

In addition to the trends of healing and prophetical challenge to society, a third key trend within this liberational thrust has been the adoption and development of new attitudes of creativity, imagination, and hope. If we are to resolve world problems, we must challenge them in new ways and offer new solutions and alternatives. Organizations, whether civil or ecclesiastical, seem dedicated above all to self-preservation, and unless the prophetical Christian can propose new and creative solutions, those structured injustices will remain.[37] Today's prophet, dedicated to liberation, must have imagination and vision, facilitated by rest, leisure, and contemplation of the Word.

Our examination of the major trends in today's spirituality reveals that spirituality now has a clear political and social dimension. Involvement in social justice issues is seen as a dimension of faith and of the will of God. The major trends in today's spirituality also show a clear return to values found in the lives of all the baptized. The emphases are ecclesial, not ecclesiastical; incarnational, not flight from the world; oriented toward service to the world, not to hierarchical ministry; liberational, not exclusively sacramental. These emphases never exclude their alternatives, but complement them.

Characteristics of Christian Spirituality

All the baptized are called to the fullness of Christian life and to one and the same holiness. Religious and priests may need to develop additional specific means to foster the style of life they have chosen, but the basic gospel-revealed characteristics of Christian life are for everyone. In short, there seems to be no need for a specifically lay spirituality. All Christians share equally the same fundamental spirituality. This spirituality is not vocationally distinct in essentials but is graded and judged exclusively on fidelity. In baptism, all are called to follow Christ in the Church. Sometimes in the history of spirituality, accidentals of Christianity have been emphasized more than essentials, and some individuals have been greatly esteemed for practices or attitudes that were not really integral to the nature of Christianity. The trends we will now discuss are concerned with major common characteristics, some of which are traditional and some of which are new priorities of recent times.

Sense of baptismal vocation

The fundamental moment of Christian life is the life received and the commitment made in Christian initiation. The whole of life is meant to be the intensification of this received life and the mature living out of this responsibility. Discipleship is the embodiment, individually and as Church, of the gifts and obligations received in baptism. For each Christian, baptism is a washing that purifies (see Eph. 5:26; Tt. 3:5; Heb. 10:22); an illumination (see Eph. 5:14; Heb. 6:4; 10:32); a new birth (see Tt. 3:5; Jn. 3:5; 1 P. 1:3; 2:2). It seals us in faith, unites us to Christ, joins us to his people. Christian initiation is the personal anointing by the Holy Spirit (see 2 Co. 1:21-22; Eph. 1:13; 4:30; 1 Jn. 2:20-27). As a result of each baptized person's rights and duties within the community, there can be no essential distinction between active and passive Christians. The Vatican Council stated this clearly: "The chosen people of God is one. . . . As members they share a common dignity from their rebirth in Christ. They have the same filial grace and the same vocation to perfection" (C 32:2). Each Christian needs a stronger sense of this baptismal vocation, which will always include a vocation to ministry (see L 2:1). Finally, fidelity to this baptismal vocation is necessary for the renewal of the Church (see E 6:1).

Having entered into this experience, or in later life having become aware of it, each one must deliberately use all appropriate means to manifest fidelity to this baptismal call, to preserve and foster it. This will include meditation on the Word, prayer, sharing with the community of faith, ongoing education, and some clearly identified involvement in ministry. Baptism permeates every dimension of one's personality in an ongoing daily conversion. One's whole approach to life must manifest awareness of this baptismal reality, which, while principally a grace accepted, must be shown in daily deliberate effort.

The other side of baptismal responsibility is Christian liberty (see Ga. 5:13-18; Rm. 6:14; 7:1-6; 8:2). One cannot exist without the other. Liberty, however, is one of the last stages attained in spiritual growth. In baptism all receive the gift of freedom and are called to live as free people in Christ (see Ga. 5:13). Because we recognize this same freedom in the other, we should sincerely appreciate the integrity of each Christian and try to remove all pseudo-moral and pseudo-religious pressures that limit freedom.

Our call to baptismal freedom also demands that we be faithful to our conscience. No one can violate our freedom by forcing us to be faithful to our baptismal call; but just as truly, we cannot pass on to someone else our responsibility to make decisions. Christianity of its very nature consists in "internal, voluntary, and free acts whereby man sets the course of his life directly toward God" (RF 3:4).

As we saw, then, the first characteristic of Christian spirituality is a sense of baptismal call, an appreciation of personal vocation. This sense of call includes a realization of belonging to the community of faith. It implies a primacy of the Word, lived with liberty and fidelity to conscience, and it includes a sense of ministry in the name of the Church.

Awareness that life is grace

Spirituality does not refer primarily to the effort and

asceticism of Christians, but rather to what God is doing in us. So a second hallmark of Christian spirituality is the awareness that life is grace, gift from God. A Trinitarian dimension must dominate all Christian spirituality. God's baptismal call to us is not just words, but gives us the power to be disciples; it is living power, utter conviction (see 1 Th. 1:5; 2:13). God the Father calls us, confirms us in holiness, makes us blameless, perfects us (see 1 Th. 3:12-13; 4:8-14). We are his children (see 1 P. 1:23); he anoints us for his glory (see 1 P. 2:9) and challenges us to be holy (see 1 P. 1:15-16). Jesus redeems us, directs us to his Father, becomes the model of our life, is the cornerstone of the Church we enter in baptism (see 1 P. 1:2; 2:21; 2:4-10). He continues to bring us fullness of life through the sacraments of the Church. Through his Spirit he sanctifies Christians in faith (see 2 Th. 2:13), makes his home within us (see Rm. 8:9; 1 Co. 3:16), gives us life, freedom, holiness and personal charisms (see Rm. 8:10; 2 Co. 3:17; 2 Th. 2:13; Ga. 5:22; 1 Co. 1:7), and guides us in ministry (see Lk. 12:12; Ga. 5:25).

This life of God within us is constantly regiven in the Church, first of all through the liturgy. The Trinitarian dimension thus becomes ecclesial and paschal. Liturgical spirituality is the spirituality of the Church. It is of its very nature Christocentric, paschal, biblical, and sacramental. No school of spirituality is more important than this essential spiritual dimension of the people. The liturgy is the individual Christian's way of participating in the history of salvation and the mystery of Christ, and it is for each one "the fount and apex of the whole Christian life" (C 11:2; see also P 6; C 3:2; 7:3). This will require ongoing education in the liturgy and constant training of both clergy and laity in order that all be actively involved. It could also require new Church structures to make such participation possible.

The Father, Son, and Holy Spirit are the very life that constitutes Christian spirituality. This life comes to us not only in the liturgical life of the Church but also in personal, individual prayer. Prayer, whether vocal, meditative, or contemplative, is open to all. Attainment of different levels of prayer is not assigned according to vocation or state. Laity must be trained to prepare for contemplative prayer and for all depths of the mystical experience.

The life and grace of God, received in baptism and fostered in liturgy and prayer, is manifested in each one through the three theological virtues of faith, hope, and charity (see 1 Th. 1:3; 5:8). These virtues manifest both the graced life of God and the Christian's lived acceptance of that life (L 4:2). They are the fundamental energies of each Christian, and in some way the whole of spiritual development is the maturing of this theological life. The very powers of human life—intellect, memory, and will—are given new orientation through Christian faith, hope, and love. The intellect through faith attains to truth; the memory plus hope arrives at a totally satisfying vision; the will aided by charity arrives at real love. "Spirituality . . . is a love which through faith and hope leads one to a greater share in existence."[38]

The second characteristic of Christian spirituality, then, is the daily lived awareness that life is grace. Growth in Christian living is principally the work of the Trinitarian Lord within us, calling us to holiness and bringing about that holiness within us through his grace, the liturgy, prayer, and the theological virtues. Just as all are called through faith and baptism, so too is life freely and fully sown in each and every baptized Christian.

Commitment to evangelical life

The third characteristic of Christian spirituality is a commitment to evangelical life, and the clearest summary of the lifestyle to which the gospel calls us is given in the Sermon on the Mount. This is the charter sermon of Christianity and is a synthesis of all the new levels of awareness and commitment to evangelical life that the disciple should have.[39] The sermon clearly indicates that Christianity has a new audience: It is a religion of all the people, especially those in need—the helpless and abandoned, those who long to be healed and cured. It is not a religion of the elite, enlightened, or religiously informed.

Christianity brings to the world a new set of values in the beatitudes. To the oppressed of society, to the have-nots, to those who constantly weep in their distress, and to those whose faith is mocked by society, Jesus brings glad tidings, proclaims liberty, healing, and release. He calls for detachment, simplicity, single-minded commitment to himself, longing for God, compassion, peacemaking, and the ability to accept the suffering that results from decisions of faith.

The Sermon on the Mount gives us the new goal of Christianity: universal love and compassion.[40] It also lists new attitudes in our daily dealing with others, particularly within the community of the Church. There should be no judging or condemning of others, no faultfinding or petty criticisms. Rather, the disciple should be a person of compassion, forgiveness, and understanding.

Finally, the charter sermon clarifies the new criteria for judging authenticity and fidelity in one's commitment. These will include quality of life, fruitfulness in ministry, obedience to the Word, and totality of self-gift to Jesus. The evangelical life presented in the Sermon on the Mount has a strong individual, social, ecclesial, and political dimension. It is a well-rounded presentation of values in which every baptized person can find a home.

It has been traditional in the Church to synthesize the gospel call not only in the charter sermon but also in the evangelical counsels. The documents of Vatican II refer to "the manifold counsels, proposed in the gospel by our Lord to His disciples" (C 42:5). These counsels as a general characteristic of Christian spirituality are dealt with in the fifth chapter of the document on the *Church*, the section on the universal call to holiness, and this is certainly a significant statement of the Church. Because the evangelical counsels, particularly poverty, chastity, and obedience, have come to be closely identified with religious life, it is important to state that we are not concerned with a lay version of religious life, nor are we referring to a living of the counsels "in spirit," if that should imply a watering down of the counsels.

Each baptized Christian is called by God and patiently lives out this call step by step in interaction with the surrounding world. These interactions are either with things or with people, individually or socially. This gives us three major relationships: with the possession of temporal goods, with people in interpersonal relationships of love, and with the structured and organized interrelationships of community.[41] Christians, single-mindedly committed to God, cannot absolutize anything but must be ever open to God alone. When one of these three relationships is absolutized, we sin by not being open to be more, to be for, or to be with. The three principal evangelical counsels challenge all Christians to live in a just relationship to things (poverty), in a just relationship of person to person (chastity), and in a just relationship of person to society (obedience).

These are the basic challenges of the counsels to which Church law has added other specifics for religious in their vows. The essentials of the challenge, however, are for all. Each is called to detachment and non-possessiveness; no one may absolutize his or her love in another person, nor be possessive of another, but must always have a chaste heart; all are called to obedience to the salvific will of God for all society. A just use of goods and a renunciation of them, a positive valuing of every human being and of sexual abstinence, obedience to God and a sacrifice of self-will are integral parts of the life of every baptized person.

This third characteristic of spirituality is for all who in faith follow Jesus. They are challenged to the fullness of the evangelical life as presented in the precepts of the Sermon on the Mount and in the counsels of Jesus in the gospel.

Openness to new priorities

Gregory of Nyssa, one of the Fathers of the Church, spoke about Christian life as a never-ending movement "from beginnings to beginnings through beginnings." This is true for each individual, rising from daily failures and beginning again. It is true also of Christian spirituality as it faces a changing world, a changing history, and a changing Church. Spirituality, which means "the personal assimilation of the salvific mission of Christ by each Christian . . ., is always in the framework of new forms of Christian conduct."[42] Today we live in a world characterized by change. The change is profound, constant, accelerated, universal, and ambivalent (see CT 5; 6; 73).

In this situation Christians are constantly faced with new ways of thinking, new ways of living, new scales of values. What are the appropriate evangelical attitudes for today? How can the message be incarnated anew so that what was spirit and life when proclaimed by Jesus will be spirit and life for us today? One of the major characteristics of Christian spirituality, then, is openness to new priorities. This does not mean that Christians always accept what is new, for some of the rigorous calls of the gospel will never change. But Christianity, looking at the signs of the times, can in faith discover the call of God in all its newness and respond to those new priorities that conform to the gospel call.

What are the priorities calling for our response today? Four major groupings of new priorities seem to form part of contemporary Christian spirituality.

The first is the hope for integral human growth manifested in desires for personal fulfillment, in quality of relationships, in a sense of wonder, in the recognition of the need for integrating sexuality into Christian growth, in longings for enriching and life-giving religious experiences. These aspirations are healthy and must be integrated into spirituality.

Secondly, today's spirituality strongly emphasizes group growth and asceticism. We see these in shared faith and prayer, in community life, in intervocational ministries, in collegial forms of government, in new forms of group leadership, in small-group liturgies, in charismatic experiences, and in ecclesial spiritual movements. This placing of priority on group growth has signaled a move away from individualistic approaches to spirituality and a redirection to communitarian approaches.

The third list of new priorities can be grouped under the yearning for the justice of faith. Nowadays, many experience God in others and in the world, and they are called to a life and ministry of world justice. In our own generation we have again arrived at the conviction of the prophets that there is no authentic spirituality without a commitment to justice.

The fourth new priority of our generation is the awareness that our commitment must include changeability and constant openness to the future. An attitude of co-responsibility for the future fosters an openness to science and discovery, a spirit of creativity, and a detachment even from the outward forms of religion. If we are to survive the constant change of our time and bring Christ's message anew to the people of each generation, then this quality of openness must also be a component of Christian spirituality.[43]

These four characteristics of spirituality—sense of baptismal vocation, awareness that life is grace, commitment to evangelical life, and openness to new priorities—are also the basic form of Christianity both as it was in the beginning and in its new presence today. In Christianity, unlike in other world religions, there is a special call or vocation for every member. There is, however, no caste-like system, for God gives the essence of the life to all without distinction. In its gospel form, Christianity is not a two-tiered morality or spirituality, but a universal call to holiness. Like Christ himself, each baptized person must be truly incarnated in the world of his or her day, sensitive to its needs and to the new aspirations of all men and women. The characteristics of Christian spirituality are an encouraging reaffirmation of the call of all the baptized.

Spirituality and Spiritualities

Having examined basic trends and characteristics of Christian spirituality, we must ask, What is the relationship between the one unchanging Christian spirituality and the many manifestations of it in personal or group spiritualities for today?

Christian spirituality is the lived integration of perennially valuable gospel teachings and the ever-changing human conditions of each generation. We must always confront our lives with the gospel message given in the past, but we live it today. The gospel call needs to be lived with freshness and relevance in every generation, since Jesus did not come only for the Palestinian Jews of two thousand years ago, but for all of us wherever and whenever we live. Hence his message must be incarnated in different cultures and different generations.

Over the centuries our concepts of God and of the human person have evolved; our notions of sacred and profane have changed; our understandings of Church and society have developed. As people gain new insights into religion, Christianity is lived out differently. Scriptures do not just give us a list of teachings to be followed or methods that will lead to religious enlightenment; rather, the New Testament is essentially the revelation of a person and how he lived his life of dedication to God. The same person appeals differently to various groups, cultures, and periods of history, and he challenges the different embodiments of the gospel call to follow him.

The one spirituality in Jesus can be lived out in many ways. This was already true in the gospels, where the challenges of discipleship were different for the suffering and persecuted Roman Church of Mark and for the Palestinian Church of Matthew afflicted with internal problems, divisions, and anxiety. This Christian spirituality has had many forms over history and still has many forms in our pluralistic age.

The terms *spirituality* and *spiritualities*

Spirituality is an evolving notion. It is one and unique in Christ, but it is lived out differently over the centuries. It is rooted in the life, example, teachings, and mission of Jesus, but each generation brings new problems, different needs, and different experiences to it. The challenge of Jesus is permanent, but the ways of living out that challenge are transitory. In Jesus we have one unique Christian spirituality, but over history we have many spiritualities, many different complementary and mutually enriching forms of the response to the gospel challenge. As conditions change, new life-styles develop, and when these can be authenticated and verified in Jesus' teachings, they are new spiritualities for the Church.

There is a well-known ikon that illustrates the variety of spiritualities. This ikon shows a bishop clothed in splendid robes talking to a poor man covered in mud. Both are saints, but their spiritualities are very different. The former chose an ecclesiastical and political incarnation of Christianity, while the latter chose one of the sacrifices current in his time. In the late twelfth and early thirteenth centuries we have Francis of Assisi and Dominic, so different in their ways of living out Jesus' call. In the fourteenth century we have several Dominicans: Eckhart, Tauler, and Suso, but how different are their spiritualities! In fifteenth-and sixteenth-century Spain we have Ignatius of Loyola, Teresa of Avila, and John of the Cross. Each spirituality in the Church must be viewed with reverence but never absolutized lest it become a block to a future reinterpretation of the call.

What accounts for the differences we see in spiritualities? Sometimes spiritualities are different because of the country of their origin; sometimes they differ because the founders lived in different psychological, cultural, or social conditions; sometimes a combination of local needs challenges persons to a specific Christian response; sometimes we can discern no immediate reason and see principally the free inspiration of the Holy Spirit.[44]

Each of these different spiritualities embodies the major elements of Jesus' revelation, and each one can be verified in Jesus' gospel challenge. The call, however, is originally actualized in a very individual and personal experience.

Generally, we are dealing with a committed Christian who, under the inspiration of the Holy Spirit and molded by the environment, responds anew in a Christlike way to local needs and circumstances. This experience of the founding personality is then appreciated by the Church, and a sort of canonical acceptance is given to the spirituality, which is then imitated by many followers who feel they live in circumstances similar to those to which the spirituality was a response. "The most fruitful spiritualities seem to grow rather out of actual Christian existence than out of ideas," and "concrete spiritualities can be grasped less as doctrine than as personal existence."[45]

As circumstances change, the Church will always need new incarnations of Christian spirituality in a variety of spiritualities. Spiritual leaders who can analyze needs and discover new ways of living out Jesus' call will always give birth to new spiritualities.

New states of life

As new spiritualities developed, they were in time submitted to Church authorities for formal official acceptance. Almost all these spiritualities arose within organized religious life, or they became the basis for a new form of religious life that was then established by the Church. Historically, all schools of spirituality that survived for any length of time were associated with clerical or religious life. Those oriented to laity have not survived in any organized form.

We have traditionally spoken of three major spiritualities that depend on vocation and state of life: the spirituality of consecrated religious life, priestly spirituality, and lay spirituality. This emphasis has done great good for the Church and has given vocational identity and challenge, particularly to the religious and priests. But in the Church today, only one half of one percent of the people are priests, and only 1.5 percent are religious.[46] In view of those statistics, the enormous emphasis given in writings to the vocational spiritualities of these two groups is certainly out of all proportion to the needs of the whole people. Admittedly, new emphasis will need to be given to these two vocational spiritualities in the near future since there is identifiable erosion of the common elements on which they are built: There are priests in ministry, priests in administration, priests in a variety of professions; there are religious who live in community, and others who maintain private apartments; there are vastly different interpretations of poverty and obedience. It is now very difficult to construct a spirituality of the priest or the religious since the common elements are understood in such a variety of ways.

When we look at the general body of the baptized, we are confronted with a major task of direction. If there is no such thing as a spirituality of the priest or religious—and it seems we are in practice arriving at that conclusion—then certainly there is no such thing as a spirituality of the laity. There is only the one unique Christian spirituality; but, just as this was lived out in a variety of ways over history, so it is lived out in a variety of ways today by laity, priests, and religious. There are married people, divorced, separated, widowed, youth, single (including those who are single because of ministry choices); there are people in business, politics, factories, service industries, personnel services, helping professions, ecclesial ministries; there are the healthy, sick, disabled; there are the baptized who live in wealthy countries or poor countries, in democracies or dictatorships, in freedom or persecution. The number in each of these categories is larger than the entire number of priests or religious in the world. Because of this and the increasing difficulty in arriving at a clerical or religious spirituality, the previous distinction into states of life is no longer of value. We need to rethink the whole notion of vocational spiritualities and establish a restructuring of spiritualities that can be relevant for the people of God in the twentieth century. The concept of vocational spirituality is good and should be maintained, but the vocations are many, and the spiritualities will be varied.

Lay spirituality

The spiritualities of all the baptized will vary according to their condition. Christian spirituality as lived by laity will be the full life of the Church. There are superficial distinctions between active and passive life-styles, missioned and instrumental ministry, sacred and secular situations, incarnation and flight, sexual life and chastity, possessions and poverty. Ecclesial life is complex, and all baptized are called at one time or another to all these manifestations of commitment and holiness (see C 41; 42).

All baptized are integral parts of the mystery of the Church. Previously it was easy to identify the role of the priest, of the religious, and of the laity, but this is not so now. While we need to preserve some essential distinctions, there is also a healthy merging and sharing of responsibilities in other spheres. Now, rather than emphasizing a ruling class, we are all called to live as Church with a sense of enthusiasm, collaboration, and co-responsibility (see C 32:4; 33:4; B 16; M 21:6).

The call to live as communion is for all levels of ecclesial life. For some the prime group will be a religious community; for others, a family. This Christian love lived and shared is then brought to the secondary structures of parish or diocese. In this ecclesial communion people are more important than institutional structures, and personal rights cannot be submerged for institutional permanence.

It has often been suggested that laity can be defined as "Christians in the world" and that their spirituality is one of "insertion in the world" (see C 31:3; L 7:5). But this seems inaccurate, since all baptized live in the world and interact with the world, and as Church all are called to be sacrament of the world. To say that priests and religious interact with the world in a formally different way does not correspond to reality. After centuries of exaggerated spiritualism we accept that no one can find fulfillment exceppt as a pilgrim in the midst of God's world. "It is in the world that a life proves itself Christian,"[47] and the Council condemned any split between the two (see CT 43:2). Each baptized person lives as the servant Church in his or her own circumstances. At times, for all, this can be within Church structures; at other times, within temporal spheres. The latter situation, however, is not exclusive to laity (see CT 43:4). All are called to be leaven; and genuinely appreciating the world in order to serve it is the task of the whole Church. Rather than say the laity has "a special competence" in this sphere, it would be more nearly accurate to say that all people live in this condition, with a few special exceptions such as hermits. All the baptized, whatever their condition, are called to be heralds of faith and witnesses to Christ and his message (see C 35; M 21:4; L 6:4; 16:1).

Lay spirituality is not qualified by "world" or "insertion" or "instrumental." Living as Church in its fullness is the only spirituality for laity. They are an integral part of the rich mystery and a dynamic part of the communion. They are an ecclesial sacrament for the world, serving it and witnessing Christ. They are the people of God, the prime Christian presence.

In this section I have not begun to specify the new vocational spiritualities we need. I am aware of initial efforts, but the field remains largely unexplored. Here I have been more concerned to stress our need to be aware that all share the major common components and that laity are challenged to fullness of Christian life. However, in our rapidly changing world we must become skilled in discerning the specific needs of people's changing conditions of life and in formulating the details of a spirituality and style of reaction to those conditions. It is now very possible that the same layperson will need several different spiritualities in the course of a lifetime. Hence we need to be trained, and we need to train others, to know the constants of Christian spirituality and to be flexible and creative in incarnating them.

Conclusion

We live in a period of considerable interest in spirituality and a time of focusing pastoral concerns on laity and their needs. Examining a spirituality of all the baptized produces much to give encouragement. The general move toward ecclesiology and toward a more integrated approach to the mystery of the Church has helped us consolidate directives for lay life today.

This was not always the case, and although we find Jesus calling all to holiness, it remains unfortunate and unquestionable that history shows a drift away from the ordinary baptized and a zeroing in on the spirituality of special groups. In fact, real scorn and disdain for the normal components of lay life was easy to discern, and a monastic spirituality imposed itself on the whole Church. The general body of the faithful was never totally abandoned, however, and some key figures and movements never ceased to affirm the gospel's call of the whole Church to holiness. This call of the whole Church has been explicitly reaffirmed in this century, particularly by the Second Vatican Council.

When we look at the trends in spirituality today, we find that they show a clear return to common values of all the baptized and specifically to a reevaluation of the positive contributions of lay life. Today, spirituality is ecclesial and incarnational; it challenges us to serve the world and to become involved in social justice issues. We are no longer dealing with unusual ascetical practices but are concentrating on the basic life-style implied in the universal baptismal vocation.

In analyzing the basic characteristics of Christian spirituality, we found a universally applicable challenge of gospel values rather than a graded or two-tiered spirituality. Each baptized person is called to the fullness of Christian life.

Finally, our reexamination of the relationship between basic Christian spirituality and its manifold incarnations in spiritualities stressed lay needs in this area and suggested that we reassess the states of life and vocational spiritualities. Much needs to be done to develop new formulations of spiritualities for work, married life, single life, divorced, youth; we need to be far more specific in developing the spiritualities of the various professions. While there is much yet to be done, the challenge holds great promise, for we are beginning a period of remarkable exploration in formulating spirituality for all the baptized.

Concluding Comments

The years ahead, particularly the next ten to fifteen, will be among the most thrilling and challenging that Christianity has lived through. They have the possibility of opening us to a newer and fresher life than any of us have ever experienced. For each one of us this next period will be one of crisis and judgment on our fidelity and our depth of commitment to the call of Jesus. We will need Christians who have this gospel challenge in their bones and who can, through an intense shared life, continually generate new energies and power for commitment and involvement for the years ahead.

In this book we have reviewed four major areas of concern for laity today. Chapter 1 synthesized developments in the theologies of laity since the Vatican Council II. In the Church today several approaches to laity coexist, and each approach has both strengths and weaknesses. Each of us approaches the multifaceted debate on the role of laity in the Church with the presuppositions, positions, and prejudices of the particular model or theology of laity we assume. This pluralism of theologies is good if we see an effort to reach a consensus on major issues. In general, the years since Vatican II look very encouraging, particularly because the question of laity has moved into the area of ecclesiology. The awareness that it is the laity's task to be Church in its fullness is already having major impact on all other developments regarding the life, role, and mission of laity.

The purpose of Chapter 2 was to evaluate the postconciliar effort to integrate the laity into the life of the universal Church. The brief survey revealed that, in spite of all the good will and sincere ecclesial commitment, the life and ministry of the laity have been severely lacking in development. This gives rise to serious concern. Structures and authority are exclusively non-lay; lay rights and duties are minimal; ecclesial collaboration is in its infancy. Spiritual renewal has been greatly emphasized since the Council, but an authentic spirituality of all the baptized has not emerged. The whole area of mission and ministry is still predominantly hierarchical and clerical. The negative evaluation of the current situation is made not only by laity but also by Church leaders, both clerical and religious. The willingness to evaluate honestly and face openly the discrimination and resulting unecclesial relationships is itself, however, a healthy development and augurs well for the future.

In Chapter 3 we set out to discern an approach to the Church that was understandable to all the people of God and that laity could immediately identify with. We emphasized the Church as a family and stressed the spiritual interrelationship between Church life and family life. Laity have much to contribute since their experiences within the foundational cells of family life are the very attitudes and convictions necessary for the growth of the universal Church. This return to an understanding of the Church that is a lay vision and non-elitist is encouraging for laity and hope-filled for the future.

Chapter 4 concentrated on formulating a spirituality of all the baptized. We saw the negative and positive developments of history culminating in a universal call to holiness in the teachings of Vatican II. In examining contemporary trends in spirituality and essential characteristics of a spirituality of all the baptized, we saw that the qualities emphasized today are the basic qualities in the daily life experience of all the baptized. This trend leads to a positive reevaluation of lay life.

Whether we look at contemporary theologies of laity or evaluate the current situation of laity in the Church or reflect on a possible consensus in our understanding of the nature of the Church or seek the impetus to growth in Christian life, the results are the same: a return to a deeper appreciation of the integral role of laity in the life and mission of the Church. This deeper appreciation has led to new approaches to corporate responsibility, discipleship, mission, and ministry. Although problems remain, there are many signs of a new direction in ecclesiology and lay life.

In the Church of recent years we have witnessed a clearly identifiable humanizing of local ecclesial structures. In many places throughout the world, parishes, interparochial groups, and dioceses have begun to decentralize and to introduce new diocesan and parochial structures: pastoral councils, parish councils, and administrative secretariats. In many ecclesial groups we have witnessed a new spirit in administration and authority, one that has led to intervocational interaction and to new forms of leadership. As we have said, corporate and structural change is rarely facilitated by top administrators in any organization; instead, growth comes from the grass-roots groups and filters upward, provoking changes in attitudes that lead to structural modifications. In today's Church, then, we see many signs of this growth-from-the-roots.

There are still serious problems, however. It is unlikely that Rome will encourage substantial decentralization, or that we will see any serious relinquishing of Roman power for the sake of national, local, or ecumenical development. Today we still have an exclusively male-dominated, ecclesiastical, multinational corporation that overemphasizes hierarchical power, jurisdiction, office, officialdom, and law.

In upgrading the image of all the baptized, we need to see a greater commitment to developing a Church of the people that lives genuine charity, community, and mutual service; that emphasizes charism, theology for all, and pluralism of life-styles; that lives humility toward fellow Catholics and non-Catholic groups within the Christian family. Major changes will be very gradual and will come from the prophetical life-styles of local groups that include genuine lay presence in policy and planning.[1]

Dissatisfaction with Church structures has led to a need for smaller groups of faith-sharing. However, even experimental forms of lay participation are not likely to persist. Many of the parish councils of today are producing not a grass-roots involvement but an administrative consolidation of a dedicated few. At all levels we must move away from the presumption that administrative or managerial positions are necessarily leadership positions. We must accept true leadership wherever we identify it. As Johannes B. Metz has expressed it, we must move "from a leadership that 'has' authority to a leadership that 'is' authority."[2] In the future, in some cases this true leadership will be found in individuals: priests, religious, or laity. In other cases it will surface in group manifestations. Each vocation will be respected, and in these times of restructuring, a special concern must be directed to preserving the leadership role of the priest in all areas of ritual, mediation, and ecclesial sanctification. In the years ahead, however, this leadership role will not extend to a monopoly over governing and teaching unless the charism is verified by the community. In addition, religious orders will have smaller numbers as the Church stresses the universality of the call to holiness.[3]

This new direction in the Church calls for simplification, decentralization, and broader ecclesial participation in Church structures. These in turn will include ecclesial living in small groups where baptismal dignity and equality are lived realities—a life-style that calls for authentic pluralistic and intervocational styles of commitment.

Discipleship will also imply in all groups, including the primary family cells, an awareness of being a community in Christ. This awareness will include interest in the group's Christian identity and a deeper sense of responsibility in faith for all other members of the family Church. This will also lead to a willingness to grow as a group in mutual acceptance, faith-sharing, personal prayer, liturgy, and common mission.

In addition to growth in community awareness, each disciple in the rapidly changing world of tomorrow will have to assume extensive responsibility in the work of evangelization, particularly regarding new ways of living out the gospel message. When frequent recourse to authority figures will be impossible, each disciple will need a well-formed conscience for creatively and faithfully making rapid decisions in daily life. As society grows less and less Christian, Church numbers decrease, and ministers are not replaced, local foundational Church groups will need to take upon themselves greater responsibility for faith. History shows that when this has happened to other religions, their members have become extremely conservative, unchanging, and an anomaly to society. If Catholic groups are to avoid this negative outcome, they will need to be constantly open to conscience, group discernment, and the signs of the times. They will also need to be rooted in God through personal contemplative prayer; to be prophetically committed to ever-new forms of the Church's ministry to the world; and, finally, to be enthusiastic in their commitment to the universal Church and its simple communal and vocational structures.

It is very likely that numbers entering the priesthood and religious life will continue to decrease and that numbers leaving will continue to increase. In fact, already in some parts of the world the real areas of growth, development, and vitality are in lay groups. This is where the common identity of Christianity is often best expressed today. The ranks of committed laity will grow, and a wider and more pluralistic approach to Christian commitment will develop. Unless we see a radical change in the discipline and administrative understanding of priesthood and religious life, it seems inevitable that a sense of vocation and commitment will be more and more often verified in lay forms rather than exclusively in the priesthood and religious life, as has been the tendency in the past. This shift will result in a deeper realization of the spirituality and ministry of all the baptized.

In answering the challenges of our time, the disciple will live out the cross of Christ, which is a permanent characteristic of Christianity, although it has constantly new manifestations. In the years ahead, disciples will experience the cross in the challenges of group asceticism, in the burdens of responsibility, in the provisional and transitory character of Christian spirituality's outward forms, in the need to change, in the lack of security and stability, and in the aloneness that responsibility for faith can bring.

Rarely has any previous generation since New Testament times seen such extensive involvement of laity in the mission and ministry of the Church. This has been facilitated locally by parish and diocesan structures; nationally and internationally, it has often been directed by one or other of the post-conciliar spiritual movements; and throughout the world we have witnessed the spontaneous growth of a sense of commitment to ministry by individuals and groups. In general these developments have been achieved with mutual respect among clergy, religious, and laity. On some occasions, though, it is undeniable that laity have "done their own thing" and ignored both the demands of ecclesial unity and the needed respect for the hierarchy of the Church. But it is equally undeniable that some members of the hierarchy have also "done their own thing," ignoring the baptismal rights of laity and preserving their private kingdoms. On the whole, however, the developments have been remarkably good. Commitment has grown, intervocational ministry has expanded, and new insights into the nature of the Church have resulted.

Many laity today who are committed to both spiritual development and theological investigation are well aware of their rights and duties in ministry. Generally, however, this is not the case; the image still frequently projected is that of a Church whose mission from Christ is entrusted to the hierarchy, not to the universal Church. This results in an inappropriate hierarchical control over ministry—a control far stricter than is required simply to manifest ecclesial unity and to preserve good order. We then have lay ministry that is delegated rather than rooted in the personal rights and obligations of baptism. Where laity have resisted this control, two parallel structures of ministry have often developed: a hierarchically controlled form and a lay-directed form. This is as unhealthy for the life of the universal Church as is a tiered approach to ministry.

Before all outward involvement in ministry comes commitment to fostering the life of the ecclesial community. To live as Church and thus portray the unity for which Christ prayed is the prime ministry. "Jesus established the Church to bear witness to God's Kingdom especially by the way his followers would live as the people of God."[4] In our world, shattered by hatred and disunity, there is a great prophetical value in calling for and manifesting union and unity. This ministry has developed enormously in many small basic ecclesial communities and family Churches. Commenting on the prophetical challenge of small groups, one theologian reflects: "I know of no instances of extraordinary Christian impact on society which have not grown out of a matrix dependent on this corporate, cell model."[5]

This ministry of union and unity needs to be seen more in the larger secondary groups of the Church: parishes and dioceses. To establish mutual appreciation and just vocational representation at these levels will be difficult, for we are dealing with attitudes formed over years and with decisions that have many political and economic implications. However, conversion at this level is crucial for the fidelity of the Church.

The Church, like any human community, is structured and needs structure. Religious life is structured, family life is structured, the priesthood is structured. Each group has a hierarchical dimension. Over history these three groups or vocations in the Church have been hierarchically interrelated, and at one time or another each of the three groups has been dominant. We need structure and leadership to be effective in ministry, and we should be committed to mutual support within the structures.

> This unity in the ministry should be especially evident in the relationship between laity and clergy as lay men and women respond to the call of the Spirit in their lives. . . . We applaud this solidarity between laity and clergy as their most effective ministry and witness to the world.[6]

This solidarity will develop only in a context of mutual respect for one another's vocation, charisms, and ministry.

Any attempt to monopolize or control will fail.
Laity today wish to be what they are baptized to be: active,
responsible, mature disciples of Christ.

> One of the chief characteristics of lay men and women
> today is their growing sense of being adult members of
> the church. Adulthood implies knowledge, experience
> and awareness, freedom and responsibility, and mutu-
> ality in relationships.[7]

Concentration on family life and on the family dimensions
of the Church is challenging Christians to take new
approaches to structures and responsibilities. Honest evaluation of current roles is stimulating the development of
true community in the Church. Teachings and praxis have
generated a variety of theological understandings of the role
of laity, and these have produced development and areas of
consensus regarding rights of participation in Church
structures, directions for spiritual growth, duties in ministry,
and awareness of the need to upgrade the image of laity.
Many people commit themselves in faith to foster these.
Others find the changes burdensome and personally
unacceptable, but in faith still commit themselves to them.
Overall, though, there is a healthy give-and-take, a willingness to change, a readiness to move over or move up or move
together.

The witness of a Church that manifests unity, a rejection
of all forms of caste and discrimination, and an ability to cut
across social and vocational barriers is of prophetical value
for today's world. Priests, religious, and laity are all "called
and gifted," and if we can successfully arouse a sense of call
in everyone and capitalize on the gifts of each, we can
anticipate a golden age for the Church.

The final reflections of the U.S. bishops in their document on laity provide a fitting conclusion to this book:

> The church is to be a sign of God's kingdom in the
> world. The authenticity of that sign depends on all the
> people: laity, religious, deacons, priests and bishops.
> Unless we truly live as the people of God, we will not be

much of a sign to ourselves or the world. We are convinced that the laity are making an indispensable contribution to the experience of the people of God and that the full import of their contribution is still in a beginning form in the post-Vatican II church.[8]

Notes

Chapter 1

1. "Chicago Declaration of Christian Concern." Full text in *National Catholic Reporter*, 20 January 1978, p. 11.
2. The *Catholic Periodical and Literature Index* lists 242 contributions in 1963-1964; 82 in 1965-1966; 72 in 1967-1968; 33 in 1969-1970; 22 in 1971-1972; 23 in 1973-1974; 34 in 1975-1976; 12 in 1977-1978; 26 in 1979-1980; 58 in 1981-1982; 28 in 1983.
3. Often people relied on major contributions of pre-Council years. These great works had helped produce conciliar teaching, but in most cases they were surpassed by the Council. I would include the following as major pre-Council writings on the laity: Oscar Callahan, *The Mind of the Catholic Layman* (New York: Scribner, 1963); Yves Congar, *Lay People in the Church* (Westminster, Maryland: Newman Press, 1957), (French original, 1951); "Ministères et laïcat dans les recherches actuelles de la théologie catholique romaine," *Verbum Caro* 71/72 (1964): 127-148; Ignace de la Potterie, "L'origine et le sens primitif du mot 'laïc,'" *Nouvelle Revue Théologique* 80 (1958): 840-853; Emile-Joseph De Smedt, *The Priesthood of the Faithful* (New York: Paulist Press, 1962); Christian Duquoc, "Signification ecclésiale du laïcat," *Lumière et Vie* 65 (1963): 73-98; Gérard Philips, *The Role of the Laity in the Church* (Notre Dame, Indiana: Fides, 1955); Donald Thorman, *The Emerging Layman: The Role of the Catholic Layman in America* (New York: Doubleday, 1957); Karel Truhlar, "Transformatio mundi et fuga mundi," *Gregorianum* 38 (1957): 406-445.
4. Richard P. McBrien, "A Theology of the Laity," *American Ecclesiastical Review* 160 (1969): 73.
5. See text of "Chicago Declaration of Christian Concern," and responses in *Commonweal* 105 (1978): 108-116.
6. An example would be Pam Bauer, "Church Not Ready for Lay Ministry," in *National Catholic Reporter*, 20 April 1979, pp. 1,

14, 24. See Henri Fesquet in *Le Monde*, 17 October 1963, quoted by C. Duquoc, p. 73.

7. See new Code of Canon Law, Canon 536; also Edward Schillebeeckx, "A New Type of Layman," *Spiritual Life* 14 (1968): 14-24.

8. See Charles Molette, "Brève Histoire de l'Action Catholique," in *Lumière et Vie* 63 (1963): 45-82.

9. Paul VI, "Allocutio iis qui interfuerunt Conventui tertio de apostolatu laicorum ex omnibus nationibus Romae habito," *Acta Apostolicae Sedis* 59 (1967): 1040-1048.

10. See "Consilium de Laicis: Directorium respiciens normas quibus Instituta Internationalia Catholica definiuntur," *Acta Apostolicae Sedis* 63 (1971): 948-956; also Canons 298-300 of the new Code.

11. See *National Catholic Reporter*, 22 April 1977, pp. 1, 31.

12. See Desmond O'Grady, "Laity Out, Clerics In," *National Catholic Reporter*, 7 January 1977, p. 2. Also Paul VI, "Address to Pontifical Council of Laity," *Osservatore Romano* (Eng. ed.), 8 September 1977, p. 8.

13. See *National Catholic Reporter*, 28 April 1978, pp. 1-3.

14. Y. Congar, *Priest and Layman* (London: Darton, Longman and Todd, 1967), p. 318.

15. See Paul VI, "Allocutio Moderatoribus ac Membris e 'Consilio de Laicis' qui octavo plenario Coetui Romae habito interfuerunt," *Acta Apostolicae Sedis* 62 (1970): 213-216.

16. Y. Congar, *Priest and Layman*, p. 310.

17. G. Philips, *The Role of the Laity in the Church* (Notre Dame, Indiana: Fides, 1955), p. 172.

18. For attitudes that the Council hopes will be developed: L 22:2; C 37:3; 32:3; L 10:1.

19. E. Schillebeeckx, "A New Type of Layman," pp. 14-24, esp. p. 20; R. McBrien, "A Theology of the Laity," p. 73; "Church," *Chicago Studies* 12 (1973): 249.

20. See Y. Congar, "Ministères et Structuration de l'Eglise," *Ministères et Communion Ecclésiale* (Paris: Editions du Cerf, 1971), p. 34.

21. See C. Duquoc, "Signification ecclésiale du laïcat," *Lumière et Vie* 65 (1963): 88, 85; see also Charles Davis, *God's Grace in History* (London: Fontana, 1967), p. 36.

22. E. Schillebeeckx, "Definizione del laico cristiano," in *La Chiesa del Vaticano II*, Guilherme Barauna, ed. (Florence: Vallecchi, 1966), p. 959.

23. The important works of Gustave Thils, *La théologie des réalitiés terrestres* (Bruges: De Brouwer, 1946; Marie-Dominique Chenu, *The Theology of Work* (Dublin: Gill and Sons, 1963); *Théologie de la matière, civilisation technique et spiritualité chrétienne* (Paris: Editions du Cerf, 1968). For a good description of erroneous theological views, see P. Charles, "Créateur des choses visibles," in *Nouvelle Revue Théologique* 67 (1940): 261-279; Gabriele Panteghini, "Il Mondo come opera di Dio e come opera del Maligno," *Il mondo materiale nel piano della salvezza* (Rome: ed. Paoline, 1968), pp. 244-248.

24. For a good explanation of the word *world* see E. Guano, *Relatio super schema De Ecclesia in mundo huius temporis* (Rome: 1964), p. 10.

25. See Y. Congar, *Lay People in the Church*; K. Rahner, "L'apostolat des Laïcs," *Nouvelle Revue Théologique* 78 (1956); E. Schillebeeckx, *The Layman in the Church* (New York: St. Paul Publications, 1963).

26. See K. Rahner, *Christian in the Marketplace* (New York: Sheed and Ward, 1966); "Sacramental Basis for the Role of the Layman in the Church," *Theological Investigations* 8 (New York: Herder & Herder, 1971); E. Schillebeeckx, "Definizione del laico cristiano"; G. Philips, *Achieving Christian Maturity* (Chicago: Franciscan Herald Press, 1966).

27. See E. Schillebeeckx, "Definizione del laico cristiano," p. 959; K. Rahner, "The Order of Redemption within the Order of Creation," in *Mission and Grace*, 1 (London: Sheed and Ward, 1966), p. 84; Richard L. Stewart, "Et renovabis faciem terrae," in *Clergy Review*, October 1964, p. 602.

28. M 15:8; L 5; see also C 30:1; 31; L 7:5; CT 43:4.

29. Concerning proper mission, see L 1:1 and commentaries; see also E. Schillebeeckx, *Layman in the Church*, pp. 43-57; for an understanding of the evolution of the definition of laity in the Vatican Council, see Schillebeeckx, "Definizione del laico cristiano," pp. 961-968. The "National Assembly of the Laity" held at Notre Dame University, 15-17 March 1979, both by the participants' life-situations and by the ideas expressed, strongly emphasized the proper mission of the laity in secular situations.

30. Y. Congar, *Priest and Layman*, p. 303; E. Schillebeeckx, *The Layman in the Church*, p. 45.

31. K. Rahner, "L'apostolat des laïcs," p. 9; also "The Theological Interpretation of the Position of Christians in the Modern

World," in *Mission and Grace* 1 (New York: Sheed and Ward, 1963), pp. 3-58.
32. See K. Rahner, "L'apostolat des laïcs," pp. 23-24. M. D. Chenu, *Theology of Work*, pp. 37 and 12; also Y. Congar, "Le role de l'Eglise dans le monde de ce temps," in *L'Eglise dans le monde de ce temps*, 2 (Paris: Les éditions du Cerf, 1967), pp. 306-328; G. Philips, "The Church in the Modern World," *Concilium* 6 (1965): 7; G. Thils, "L'activité humaine dans l'univers," in *L'Eglise dans le monde de ce temps* 2, pp. 291-293; reaction against sin situations in today's world, see Paul VI, *Ecclesiam Suam*, 1964, part 2; Dominique Dubarle, "L'Eglise et le monde: harmonie ou divorce," in *Vie Spirituelle* 78 (1948): 627-637.
33. See Y. Congar, "Ministères et laïcat dans les rechérches actuelles de la théologie catholique romaine," p. 135; "Mon Chéminement dans la Théologie du laïcat et des ministères," in *Ministères et Communion Ecclésiale*, p. 30; E. De Smedt, "Il sacerdozio dei fedeli," in *La Chiesa del Vaticano II*, pp. 460-461; H. Symanowski, *The Christian Witness in an Industrial Society* (London: Collins, 1966), p. 113.
34. See José-Marie Gonsalez Ruiz, "A Spirituality for a Time of Uncertainty," in *Concilium* 19 (1966); H. Kelly, "The Asceticism of the Modern Apostolate," in *Doctrine and Life*, July 1967, pp. 357-358; see also CT 43:2.
35. See Albert Dondeyne, *La Fede in Ascolto del mondo* (Assisi: Cittadella, 1966), pp. 60-62; R. Stewart, p. 601.
36. See M. D. Chenu, *Theology of Work*, p. 77.
37. See particularly the criticisms of G. Philips, *Achieving Christian Maturity*, pp. 177-191, 28; Y. Congar, "Ministères et laïcat dans les recherches actuelles," p. 136; R. McBrien, "A Theology of the Laity," pp. 73-86.
38. Johannes B. Metz, *Theology of the World* (New York: Herder and Herder, 1969), pp. 101-102; see C 36:6; CT 57:1; 36.
39. Concerning methodology, see Maurizio Flick, "Riflessioni metodologiche per una teologia del Progresso," *Civiltà Cattolica* 120 (1969): 127-128; concerning scripture, see John G. Gibbs, "Pauline Cosmic Christology and Ecological Crisis," *Journal of Biblical Literature* 90 (1971): 475-479; Juan Alfaro, "Tecnopolis e Cristianesimo," *Civiltà Cattolica* 120 (1969): 533-548; M. Flick, "Costruttori del mondo e pellegrini nel mondo," in *Civiltà Cattolica* 116 (1965): 218-227; and the excellent pre-Council article: Stanislas Lyonnet, "La rédemption

de l'univers," *Lumière et Vie* 48 (1960): 43-62; concerning Christology, see B. de Margerie, "Le Christ, la sécularisation et la consécration du monde," *Nouvelle Revue Théologique* 91 (1969): 370-394; Helmut Riedlinger, "How Universal Is Christ's Kingship?" *Concilium* 11 (1966): 107-127; concerning spirituality, see J. Comblin, "Hacia una teología de la acción," *Annales de la Facultad de Teología de la Universidad de Chile*, No. 14 (1962); Jerome Hamer, "The Lay Apostolate as a State of Life," in *The Church Is a Communion* (New York: Sheed and Ward, 1964), pp. 148-153; John Paul II, *Redemptor Hominis*, 8 and 15.

40. L 7:1; C 36.

41. See H. Riedlinger, pp. 116-127; Jean-Marie R. Tillard, "La Chiesa e i valori terrestri," *La Chiesa nel mondo di oggi*, G. Barauna, ed. (Florence: Vallechi, 1966), p. 216; J. Hamer, pp. 148-153.

42. See M. D. Chenu, "I Laici e la consecratio mundi," *La Chiesa nel mondo di oggi* (Florence: Vallecchi, 1966), pp. 984. In the Council texts, see C 36; 42; 11; L 19; C 38; CT 2:2; L 5; CT 34:1; 57:2; C 31; 34. See also J. Alfaro, p. 539.

43. See H. F. R. Catherwood, *The Christian in Industrial Society* (London: Tyndale Press, 1964); CO 3; C 31; B 12:2; CT 62:8; also Alfons Auer, *Open to the World* (Baltimore: Helicon Press, 1966), pp. 312-331; Pietro Brugnoli, *Missione dei Laici nel mondo di oggi* (Brescia: Morcelliana, 1967), pp. 135-138; E. Schillebeeckx, *God and the Future of Man* (London: Sheed and Ward, 1969), pp. 78-79; J. Comblin, p. 97; Louis L'Emery, "Expérience de la foi dans l'action politique," *Vie Spirituelle* 580 (1971): 296.

44. John Paul II, Opening Address at the Puebla Conference, III, 7, in *Puebla and Beyond*, John Eagleson and Philip Scharper, eds. (New York: Orbis Books, 1979).

45. See G. Thils, "L'activité humaine dans l'univers," p. 284; Mark G. McGrath, "Note storiche sulla Costituzione," *La Chiesa nel mondo di oggi*, p. 154; E. Schillebeeckx, "The Church and Mankind," *Concilium* 1 (1965): 42; E. F. Docherty, "Personality and Perfection," *Doctrine and Life*, January 1967, p. 3.

46. Josef Ernst, "The Significance of Christ's Eucharistic Body for the Unity of Church and Cosmos," *Concilium* 40 (1968): 113-116; see Victor Warnach, "Symbol and Reality in the Eucharist," *Concilium* 40 (1968): 95-102; B. de Margerie, pp. 385-386.

47. See John Paul II, Puebla Address, III, 7.
48. See John Paul II, Puebla Address, I, 8. CT 59:1; see Teresa Margaret, "Prayer in the Secular City," *Spiritual Life* 19 (1968): 72-84.
49. See Emmanuel Mesthene, "Religious Values in the Age of Technology," *Concilium* 36 (1967): 58; E. F. Docherty, p. 4.
50. See Y. Congar, "Ministères et Structuration de l'Eglise," pp. 31-49; see also "Ministères et Laïcat dans les recherches actuelles," pp. 127-148.
51. See Y. Congar, "Mon Cheminement dans la théologie du laïcat et des ministères," pp. 22-23; R. McBrien, "Call to Action Reflects the People of God Image," in *National Catholic Reporter*, 12 November 1976; *The Remaking of the Church: An Agenda for Reform* (New York: Harper and Row, 1973). Pope John Paul II, in his encyclical, *Redemptor Hominis*, no. 5, himself applies the spirit of collegiality also to lay organizations.
52. See Jean Paul Déloupy, "Promotion du laïcat et sacerdoce," *Nouvelle Revue Théologique* 100 (1978): 20.
53. Obviously, there are serious theological problems that must be considered. See K. Rahner, "Democracy in the Church?" *The Month*, September 1968, pp. 105-119; E. Schillebeeckx, "The Catholic Understanding of Office in the Church," *Theological Studies* 69 (1969): 567-587.
54. *The Shape of the Church to Come* (New York: The Seabury Press, 1974), chaps. 3 and 4 of part 2, and 3 and 4 of part 3.
55. R. McBrien, "Church," *Chicago Studies* 12 (1973): 250.
56. See Otto Ter Reegen, "The Rights of the Laity," *Concilium* 38 (1968): 17-30. The writer speaks of rights to dialogue and discussion of ecclesiastical government in functions, administration, and grievances. Hans Küng, "Participation of the Laity in Church Leadership and in Church Elections," *Journal of Ecumenical Studies* 6 (1969): 511-533; David O'Brien, "The Ministerial Church: Realism and Responsibility," *Chicago Studies* 16 (1977): 163-168; Bernard Häring, "The Authority Crisis in Today's World," *A Theology of Protest* (New York: Farrar, Straus, and Giroux, 1970), pp. 95-117.
57. See B. Häring, "The Authority Crisis in Today's World"; Anna Morawska, "Introduction to a Theology for Laymen," *Cross Currents* 17 (1967): 5-14; editorial, *Chicago Studies* 16 (1977): 16; François Coudreau, "Lay Responsibility in the Church's Theological Mission," *Lumen Vitae* 28 (1973): 609-636; Y. Congar, "Ministères et Structuration de l'Eglise," pp. 43-45.

58. Robert A. Brungs, *A Priestly People* (New York: Sheed and Ward, 1968), p. x. For resulting details of life and ministry, see also: E. De Smedt, *The Priesthood of the Faithful*; "Priesthood of All Believers," in *Council Speeches of Vatican II*, pp. 25-27; Timothy McCarthy, *The Postconciliar Christian: The Meaning of the Priesthood of the Laity* (New York: Kenedy, 1967), chap. 5; C. Bridel, "La mission du laïcat," *Verbum Caro* 71/72 (1964): 288-311. For resulting unity of this vision, see Y. B. Tremel, "L'Eglise dans le monde," in *Lumière et Vie* 65 (1963): 22-36.

59. See Y. Congar, "Ministères et laïcat dans les recherches actuelles," pp. 127-148; J. H. Nicolas, "Les laïcs et l'annonce de la parole de Dieu," *Nouvelle Revue Théologique* 93 (1971): 821-848; Jan van Cauwelaert, "The Ordination of the Lay People to Ministries in the Church," *Lumen Vitae* 26 (1971): 585-592.

60. It is interesting to compare this with St. Paul's approach to ministry: see P. Bonnard, "Ministères et laïcat chez Saint Paul," *Verbum Caro* 71/72 (1964): 56-66.

61. See C. Bridel, pp. 288-311.

62. William J. Kelly, "Reflections on the Status of a Theology of the Layman," *Theological Studies* 28 (1967): 707.

63. See W. Kelly, pp. 706-732.

64. See "Priest Crisis Means New Ministries," *National Catholic Reporter,* Special Report II (12 May 1978), pp. 1-4.

65. See Marcel Uylenbroeck, "Lay Associations in the Church," *Osservatore Romano* (Eng. ed.), 18 August 1977, p. 8.

66. Gustavo Gutierrez, "Notes for a Theology of Liberation," *Theological Studies* 31 (1970): 244-245; see H. Sanks and B. Smith, "Liberation Ecclesiology: Praxis, Theory, Praxis," *Theological Studies* 38 (1977): 3-38.

67. One such attempt could be Roger D. Haight, "Mission: The Symbol for Understanding the Church Today," *Theological Studies* 37 (1976): 620-649.

68. See Y. Congar, "What Belonging to the Church Has Come to Mean," *Communio* 4 (1977): 146-160.

69. G. Gutierrez, "Notes for a Theology of Liberation," p. 255.

70. See R. McBrien, "A Theology of Laity," p. 73.

71. E. Schillebeeckx, *God and the Future of Man*, p. 73.

72. E. Schillebeeckx, "A New Type of Layman," p. 18.

73. Editorial, "For Clergy, Read Laity," *Clergy Review,* February 1977, p. 43; see W. Kelly, p. 721; K. Truhlar, "The Earthly Cast of the Beatitudes," *Concilium* 39 (1968): 33-43.

74. See L 1; 3:1; C 33:2.
75. Y. Congar, *Lay People in the Church*, p. xvi. This seems to be implicitly the position of John Paul II in *Redemptor Hominis*. There seem to be few vocational statements. Rather, the whole encyclical seems to be for everyone—the Church.
76. See Lucas Moreira Nevas, "A Layperson in a Vast World," *Osservatore Romano* (Eng. ed.), September 1977, p. 8; Patrick A. O'Boyle, Archbishop of Washington, D.C., "The Spirituality of the Social Apostolate," *Catholic Mind* 65 (May 1967): 37-41; L. 2:2; 9:1.
77. See L 25:1; CT 43:5.

Chapter 2

1. See Thomas W. Gillespie, "The Laity in Biblical Perspective," *Theology Today* 36 (1979-1980): 315.
2. C, chaps. 2, 4-5; L; CT; M.
3. Pope Paul VI, *On the Development of Peoples* 26 (March 1967); Latin American Episcopal Conference, *Medellín Documents*, 6 September 1968; Synod of Bishops, *Justice in the World*, 30 November 1971.
4. See François Coudreau, "Lay Responsibility in the Church's Theological Mission," *Lumen Vitae* 28 (1973): 619.
5. Hans Küng, *The Church* (New York: Sheed and Ward, 1967), p. 198.
6. See Robert C. Dixon and Dean R. Hoge, "Models and Priorities of the Catholic Church as Held by Suburban Laity," *Review of Religious Research* 20 (1979): 150-167.
7. Cardinal Wright's letter that set up pastoral councils seems to have intended this lack of lay power. See Michael Walsh, S.J., "Second-Class Citizens of the Kingdom," *Month*, November 1971, pp. 142-144.
8. An example of these difficulties was provided by the problems of lay participation in Good Shepherd parish, Arlington, Virginia. The final stage came after the death of the pastor. See "Bishop Rejects Lay Role at Pastor's Funeral," *National Catholic Reporter*, 15 February 1980, p. 43.
9. Some U.S. bishops have tried to establish due process. See Bishop James Niedergeses of Nashville, Tenn., "Governing a Local Church," reprinted in *Origins* 9 (1980): 637-641; also Bishop William Cosgrove of Belleville, Ill., "Resolving

Disputes in the Church," *Origins* 11 (1981): 3-8.
10. The opposite was the case in the early Church, as is shown by Jakob Speigl, "Lay Participation in Early Church Councils," *Theology Digest* 28 (1980): 142.
11. See James J. DeBoy, "Clergy vs. Laity: Must Authority Be Preordained?" *U.S. Catholic*, September 1980, pp. 32-34.
12. DeBoy, p. 32.
13. The Synod of Dutch Bishops in Rome would seem to have been an example of this. Its documents presented a very vertical hierarchical and legalistic view of authority. They portrayed a return to a pre-Vatican II ecclesiology and implied a put-down of laity. See Jacques Mulders, "After the Dutch Synod," *The Month*, June 1980, pp. 189-194.
14. Dixon and Hoge, pp. 165-166.
15. K. Rahner, *The Shape of the Church to Come* (New York: The Seabury Press, 1972), p. 57. See also Donald Nicodemus, *The Democratic Church* (Milwaukee: Bruce, 1968).
16. See Nicodemus, p. 40.
17. Niedergeses, p. 641.
18. See Rosemary Ruether, "Matters Left Unsaid," *Commonweal* 105 (1978): 113.
19. "Open Letter to Cardinal Ratzinger," *National Catholic Reporter*, 23 November 1979, p. 1.
20. See Niedergeses and especially Cosgrove; also Archbishop William Borders of Baltimore, "Collegiality in the Local Church," in *Origins* 9 (1980): 509-513.
21. Cosgrove, p. 3.
22. See Cosgrove, p. 1.
23. See O. Ter Reegen, "The Rights of the Laity," *Concilium* 38 (1968): 19-30.
24. Ramon Arnau, "Lay Participation in Choosing Ministers," *Theology Digest* 28 (1980): 137-142.
25. See U.S. Bishops' Committee on the Parish, "The Parish: A People, a Mission, a Structure," *Origins* 10 (1981): 645.
26. See Richard A. McCormick, "The Magisterium: A New Model," *America*, 27 June 1970, pp. 674-676.
27. Margaret Williams, "Apostolic Contemplation," *Way Supplement*, no. 7 (1969), p. 97.
28. DeBoy, p. 32.
29. *The Renewal of American Catholicism* (New York: Oxford University Press, 1972), p. 262.
30. R. McBrien, "Church," *Chicago Studies* 12 (1973): 250.

31. Unfortunately, in the past some movements of spiritual renewal with strong lay participation ended in heresy. Such was the case with the Beguines, the Brethren of the Common Life, and the disciples of Peter Waldo. In our times we must avoid this by a clear commitment to adult education.

32. See R. Kevin Seasoltz, "Contemporary American Lay Movements in Spirituality," *Communio* 6 (1979): 339-364.

33. See *Message of the Canadian Bishops: Charismatic Renewal* (Ottawa: Publication Service Canadian Catholic Conference, 1975).

34. Examples of "recent" publications which actually predate the Vatican Council would be: Alfons Auer, *Open to the World: An Analysis of Lay Spirituality* (Baltimore: Helicon Press, 1966), whose original edition in German was published in 1960; G. Philips, *Achieving Christian Maturity* (Chicago: Franciscan Herald Press, 1966), originally published in 1962.

35. L 4:7.

36. See "Redemptor Hominis," *Origins* 8 (1979), part 3; David Steindl-Rast, "The Environment as Guru," *Cross Currents* 24 (1974): 148-153.

37. See Langdon Gilkey, *Catholicism Confronts Modernity* (New York: The Seabury Press, 1975).

38. See Pierre Delooz, "The Social Function of the Canonization of Saints," *Concilium* 129 (1979): 21.

39. See R. D. Haight, "Mission: The Symbol for Understanding the Church Today," pp. 620-649.

40. See C 33; L 16:1, 3:1, 15; M 11:1.

41. See C 12:3; L 3:3, 4:7, 30:6; also Ga. 3:27-28; Eph. 4:11-13; 1 Co. 12:4-6.

42. See M 36:3; C 31, 35; L 6.

43. See L 11; C 35; CT 48, 52; Ed 3.

44. See L 13, 14; CT 4, 23, 26, 53, 60, 63-64, 75.

45. See L 7.

46. See L 10, 17, 26.

47. Regarding the general call to laity, see John Paul II, "The Role of the Laity in Africa," *Origins* 10 (1980): 47.

48. See J. van Cauwelaert, "The Ordination of the Lay People to Ministries in the Church," *Lumen Vitae* 26 (1971): 585-592.

49. See "Address to Lay Church Workers," *Origins* 10 (1980): 394.

50. U.S. Bishops' National Advisory Council, "The Thrust of Lay Ministry," *Origins* 9 (1980): 623.

51. Robert Kinast, "The Laity, a Theological Perspective," in *To*

Build and Be Church (Washington, D.C.: Bishops' Committee on the Laity, 1979), p. 7.

52. Thomas Allen, "Diaconate, Catechumenate, Lay Ministry: Three Elements of a Total Ministry," p. 25.
53. See especially C 18:1; L 24:5.
54. See C 37:3; L 25:3.
55. M 21:1; also L 1:2.
56. See C 37:1; L 3:3; M 28:1.
57. See Eph. 2:15-16; Rm. 12:3-5; Phil. 2:4; 1 Jn. 2:20, 27; 1 Pt. 3:15.
58. See, for example: Pope John Paul II, "The Role of the Laity in Africa," p. 47; "Address to Lay Church Workers," p. 393; Bishop Howard J. Hubbard of Albany, "We Are His People: A Pastoral Letter," 21 September 1978, reprinted in *To Build and Be Church*; U.S. Bishops' Committee on the Parish, "The Parish: A People, a Mission, a Structure," *Origins* 10 (1981): 645.
59. For a good, practical guide to new ministries based in very sound theology and expressed simply with abundant examples, see: Dennis Geaney, *Emerging Lay Ministries* (Kansas City: Andrews and McMeel, Inc., 1979); Council of European Bishops' Conference, "The Responsibilities of European Christians," *Origins* 10 (1980): 268-272; T. McCarthy, *The Postconciliar Christian: The Meaning of the Priesthood of Laity* (New York: Kenedy, 1967), ch. 5.
60. Juliana Casey, "Maria's Story," *Chicago Studies* 18 (1979): 17-28.
61. Brian T. Joyce, "Ministers and Ministries: A View from the Priests' Senates," *To Build and Be Church*, p. 23.
62. Examples of this could be the emphasis on the need of laity to be involved in temporal realities, or the bishops' need that laity reach the unchurched. For the latter, see "Laity Group Find They Don't Know One Another," *National Catholic Reporter*, 28 April 1978.
63. Editorial, *Chicago Studies* 16 (1977): 164.
64. Regarding women in the Church, some efforts have been made. See Archbishop Peter Gerety of Newark, "Women in the Church," *Origins* 10 (1981): 587; Archbishop Raymond Hunthausen of Seattle, *Northwest Progress*, 1 September 1980.
65. "Address to Lay Church Workers," *Origins* 10 (1980): 394.
66. Arthur Jones, "Bishops: Laity Invisible to the World," *National Catholic Reporter*, 30 March 1979, p. 12.

67. Jones, p. 14.
68. See L 3:2, 8:1, 16:6; M 11:3.
69. See M. Uylenbroeck, "Lay Associations in the Church," *Osservatore Romano* (Eng. ed.), 18 August 1977, p. 8.
70. See, for example: H. Jessup, "90 Forgotten of Boston Try Action for Recognition," *National Catholic Reporter,* 28 January 1977, p. 3; "Ex-extraordinary Minister, Priest at Odds over her Parish Duties," *National Catholic Reporter,* 20 May 1977, p. 3; also Rosemary Ruether, "Matters Left Unsaid," *Commonweal* 105 (1978): 113.
71. See Suzanne Elsesser, "Full-Time Lay-Ministers in the Church," *Origins* 10 (1980): 145-151.
72. Pope John Paul II discusses this problem of routine in "Address to Lay Church Workers," p. 392.
73. I have often asked local diocesan leaders what percentage of laity who work in the diocese and are paid by the diocese see their job as a ministry. I have never been given a figure higher than 15 percent. This included education, social services, administration, etc.
74. See Elsesser, pp. 148-149.
75. See Elsesser, pp. 149-151.
76. See Eugene Hemrick, "Need to Define Roles," *Origins* 10 (1980): 151. According to Hemrick, over 50 percent of the people working in the Church have no role description!
77. See Thomas J. Lynch, "Labor Unions in Catholic Institutions," *Origins* 10 (1980): 363-365.
78. CT 31:4.
79. Dixon and Hoge, p. 165.
80. *Frontiers for the Church Today* (New York: Oxford University Press, 1973), p. xii.
81. Alvin Toffler, *Future Shock* (London: Pan Books, 1973), p. 12.
82. Patrick Lally, "NAL or Never for Laity," *Commonweal* 86 (1967): 437.
83. James Walsh, Introduction, "Theology of Obedience," *Supplement to the Way* 5 (February 1968): 3.
84. Lynch, p. 365.
85. E. Schillebeeckx, *God the Future of Man* (New York: Sheed and Ward, 1969), p. 61.
86. See Häring, "The Authority Crisis in Today's World," in *A Theology of Protest,* pp. 95-117.
87. See Robert Brungs, *A Priestly People* (New York: Sheed and Ward, 1968), pp. 154-159.

88. See Avery Dulles, *The Resilient Church*, chaps. 5 and 6.
89. See Dulles, pp. 117-127.
90. See J. Remy, "Fault and Guilt in the Perspective of Sociology," *Concilium* 61 (1971): 16-21.
91. For an excellent study of the historical development of the lay role in preaching the word, see: J. H. Nicolas, "Les laïcs et l'annonce de la parole de Dieu," *Nouvelle Revue Théologique* 93 (1971): 821-848.
92. E. Schillebeeckx, "A New Type of Layman," pp. 14-24.
93. John Cogley, "A Good Word for the Marketplace," *The Layman and the Council*, Michael J. Greene, ed. (Springfield, Illinois: Templegate, 1964), p. 41.
94. See Langdon Gilkey, *Catholicism Confronts Modernity* (New York: The Seabury Press, 1975), p. 15.
95. See Dolores R. Leckey, "Looking at Lay Ministry: Historically, Practically, Theologically," in *To Build and Be Church*, p. 19.
96. L. Gilkey, p. 30.
97. Bernard Lee, *The Becoming of the Church* (New York: Paulist Press, 1974.), p. 286.

Chapter 3

1. *Redemptor Hominis*, no. 3.
2. *Redemptor Hominis*, no. 3.
3. Leo XIII and social reform; Pius X and liturgical renewal; Benedict XV and the renewal of law; Pius XI and both the missions and the lay apostolate; the great encyclicals of Pius XII; the conciliar work of John XXIII; and Paul VI's commitment to implementing the conciliar teachings.
4. *Models of the Church* (New York: Doubleday and Co., Inc., 1974).
5. Dulles, p. 21.
6. See A. Dulles, "Imaging the Church for the 1980's," *Thought* 56 (1981): 124.
7. See R. D. Haight, "Mission: The Symbol for Understanding the Church Today," *Theological Studies* 37 (1976): 620-649; Robert T. Sears, "Trinitarian Love as Ground of the Church," pp. 652-679 of the same issue.
8. "Imaging," p. 126.
9. "Imaging," p. 136.
10. See George Tavard, "Is There a Catholic Ecclesiology?"

Catholic Theological Society of America Proceedings, 1974, pp. 367-380.

11. *Models,* p. 26.
12. See Heribert Muhlen, *Una mistica persona* (Rome: Città Nuova Editrice, 1968), ch. 3.
13. A. Auer, *Open to the Word,* p. 266; John Paul II, "Apostolic Exhortation on the Family," *Origins* 11 (1981): 447: "Serving Life."
14. Auer, p. 273.
15. See C 31; 32; CT 44; C 7:4; 13:3. See especially John Paul II, "Exhortation—Family," pp. 453-455: "Sharing in the Life and Mission of the Church."
16. (London: Fontana, 1974), p. 280.
17. Thomas W. Gillespie, "The Laity in Biblical Perspective," in *The New Laity,* Ralph Bucy, ed. (Waco, Texas: Word Books, 1978), p. 32.
18. Not even the Vatican Council II can be the starting point. See E. Schillebeeckx, "A New Type of Layman," *Spiritual Life* 14 (1968): 18: "It is understandable that the Council, weighted down by a centuries-old tradition, was unable to arrive at a theological definition of the Christian layman. It chose the easier—and theologically less relevant—route of phenomenological description. A positive content for the ecclesial concept of layman was in fact not given."
19. In the years immediately before the Council, attempts at defining the role of laity set out from a hierarchical and clerical view of the Church. Laity appeared as second-class citizens even in Y. Congar's great attempt to liberate them: See *Lay People in the Church,* chap. 1. R. McBrien, in "A Theology of the Laity," *American Ecclesiastical Review* 160 (1969): 73, criticized some explanations in which "the Church could enjoy an integral though inadequate existence even if there were no 'lay people' within it." C. Duquoc puts the roles in perspective: "One must understand the role of the hierarchy as internal to the mission of the whole Church, and not define the Church's mission in light of the hierarchy's role." See "Signification ecclésiale du laïcat," p. 88.
20. In the years of the Council this secular quality of lay life was the predominant element in any definition. See E. Schillebeeckx, "Definizione del laico cristiano," pp. 959-977; Y. Congar, "Ministères et laïcat dans les recherches actuelles de la théologie catholique romaine," p. 135; *Priest and Layman,* p. 303; Paul VI, "Allocutio Moderatoribus ac Membris e 'Con-

silio de Laicis' qui octavo plenario Coetui Romae habito inter-
fuerunt," *Acta Apostolicae Sedis* 62 (1970): 214. See also *Documents of Vatican II*, C 30; 31; L 7; M 15:5; 21:2.
21. C. Duquoc, "Signification ecclésiale du laïcat," p. 85, insists
that laity must be free in this work and not restricted by a
hierarchical mandate.
22. See G. Philips, *Achieving Christian Maturity*, p. 28: "A positive
definition cannot be based upon a particular task which the
laity are called upon to fulfill in the world, because this would
immediately bring us outside the realm of the Church, and
the layman is by definition a member of the Church." The
specific tasks of ministry are not important, but the fact that
ministry is an integral part of the life of all the baptized is.
23. The Council already saw that this would require special formation in laity: L 29:1.
24. See E. Schillebeeckx, "Definizione," pp. 963-968.
25. See David M. Thomas, *The Prophetic Role of the Christian Family:
A Proposal for the Foundational Church*, a document prepared
for the Pre-Synod Consultation, University of Notre Dame,
15-18 June 1980.
26. Opening homily for the Synod on the Family, 26 September
1980, in *Origins* 10 (1980): 259.
27. D. Thomas, p. 6.
28. See Donald B. Conroy, *The Development of a Pastoral Approach
to Family Ministry Based on an Emerging Ecclesiology of the Christian Family*, prepared for Pre-Synod Consultation, University
of Notre Dame, 15-18 June 1980.
29. John Paul II as quoted by D. Thomas, pp. 6-7, in his synthesis
of some of the recent statements of the pope.
30. Thomas, p. 7; also Pope John Paul II, "Exhortation—Family,"
p. 451: "Relations with Other Educating Agents."
31. For a series of interesting articles and reactions, see Mitch and
Kathy Finley's column, "Family," in *Modern Ministries*, May to
September 1981. Although the prime ecclesial groups are lay
foundational Church, the universal Church does not recognize this in practice. Rather, the focal point of Church in
structure, worship, teaching, and ministry is outside of foundational Church and seems to portray a conviction that real-
life values are not to be found in the basic cells. Resulting
pastoral problems are addressed by the Finleys in their
November column and by Conroy, p. 21.
32. Dulles, "Imaging the Church," p. 121.

33. See Dulles, "Imaging," p. 123. John Paul II, showing how the ordinary Christian fits in, identifies four tasks that are at the same time family and ecclesial ministries: 1) forming a community of persons; 2) serving life; 3) participating in the development of society; 4) sharing in the life and mission of the church. See "Exhortation—Family," pp. 443-458.

34. In paragraph 9 of the Vatican Council's document on *Priests*, there is a clear attempt to redefine the priest's office of father and teacher. With the evolution of society, this family role has changed. Similar changes can be seen in C 37. See also *Spiritual Renewal of the American Priesthood*, Ernest E. Larkin, ed. (Washington, D.C.: USCC, 1973), p. 16.

35. See Tavard, "Is There a Catholic Ecclesiology?" pp. 367-380.

36. One book that has attempted an ascending approach is Bernard Besret, *Tomorrow a New Church* (New York: Paulist Press, 1973).

Chapter 4

1. The first developments of the biblical movement, with its eventual challenges in biblical spirituality, can be identified around the time of the First World War. Liturgical developments were initiated by Lambert Beaudin in 1909. Pius X's first call for lay spirituality was in 1905. The first recent commitments to ecumenism were in 1910.

2. The following contain major challenges in Christian spirituality: Leo XIII, *The Worker's Charter* (Rerum Novarum), 1891; Pius XI, *Christian Marriage* (Casti Connubii), 1930; *The Social Order* (Quadragesimo Anno), 1931; Pius XII, *The Mystical Body of Jesus Christ* (Mystici Corporis Christi), 1943; *Christian Worship* (Mediator Dei), 1947; *The Lay Apostolate* (Address to the Second World Congress on the Lay Apostolate), 1957; *World Peace and Church Freedom* (Meminisse Juvat), 1958; John XXIII, *Truth, Unity and Peace* (Ad Petri Cathedram), 1959; *New Light on Social Problems* (Mater et Magistra), 1961; *A Call to Unity* (Aeterna Dei Sapientia), 1961; *Peace on Earth* (Pacem in Terris), 1963; Paul VI, *The Church in the Modern World* (Ecclesiam Suam), 1964; *The Development of Peoples* (Populorum Progressio), 1967; *The Regulation of Birth* (Humanae Vitae), 1968; John Paul II, *Redeemer of Man* (Redemptor Hominis), 1979; *Rich in Mercy* (Dives in Mis-

ericordia), 1980; *On Human Work* (Laborem Exercens), 1981.

3. See Josef Sudbrack, "Spirituality," in *Sacramentum Mundi*, K. Rahner, ed., vol. 6, pp. 148-149; also Nicolas Berdyaev, "Salvation and Creativity: Two Understandings of Christianity," in *Western Spirituality*, Matthew Fox, ed. (Santa Fe: Bear and Co., 1981), p. 129.

4. See A. Auer, *Open to the World*, pp. 334-335.

5. Descriptive definitions will be found in Joseph De Guibert, *The Theology of the Spiritual Life* (London: Sheed and Ward, 1956), pp. 3-14; Sudbrack, pp. 148-167; Adrian van Kaam, *In Search of Spiritual Identity* (Denville, New Jersey: Dimension Books, 1975), pp. 7-13; C. Duquoc, Preface, *Concilium* 9 (1965): 1-3.

6. Katherine Dyckman and L. Patrick Carroll, *Inviting the Mystic, Supporting the Prophet* (New York: Paulist Press, 1981), p. 79.

7. "Tendencies of Contemporary Spirituality," *Concilium* 9 (1965): 26.

8. Y. Congar, *Lay People in the Church*, p. 2: "We see then that there is no distinction between 'lay-people' and 'clerics' in the vocabulary of the New Testament."

9. I mention again that etymologically the word *laity* means "people of God." It is possible, then, to say that Jesus preached a spirituality for all laity.

10. See Leonard Doohan, *Luke: The Perennial Spirituality* (Santa Fe: Bear and Co., 1982), chap. 6, "Call of Discipleship."

11. See the references in A. Auer, *Open to the World*, chap. 1: "Lay Spirituality in Early Christian Times."

12. Auer, p. 37, quotes Gregory Nazianzen: "The contemplative life is for those few who are perfect, the active life is for everyone else."

13. See "The First Epistle of Clement to the Corinthians," and "The Epistles of Ignatius," in *Early Christian Writings* (Harmondsworth, England: Penguin Books, 1968), pp. 15-132.

14. Jean Guitton, in *The Church and the Laity* (Staten Island, New York: Alba House, 1965), reports that John Henry Cardinal Newman saw the role of laity in these early times as very positive. In fact, Newman suggested that laity were the only supporters of Bishop Athanasius against Arianism.

15. See the synthesis and comments of Jean Leclercq, *The Spirituality of the Middle Ages* (New York: The Seabury Press, 1968), pp. 7-8. This is vol. 2 of *The History of Christian Spirituality*, Jean Leclercq, François Vandenbroucke, and Louis Bouyer, eds.

16. See Leclercq, p. 10.
17. See Leclercq, chaps. 4, 5.
18. See Leclercq, p. 174.
19. See Leclercq, pp. 499-505.
20. St. Francis de Sales, *Introduction to the Devout Life* (London: Burns and Oates, 1962), p. 1.
21. Louis Gognet, *Post-Reformation Spirituality* (New York: Hawthorn Books, 1959), p. 63.
22. Legion of Mary (1921), Focolare (1943), Cursillo de Cristiandad (1949), Movement for a Better World (1945); family movements such as Equipes Notre Dame (1949), Movimiento Familiar Cristiano (1950), Domus, Cana; movements of social and political involvement such as Opus Dei (1928). Every country seems to have witnessed popular spiritual movements: Action 365 (Germany), Graal (Holland), Oasi (Italy), Schoenstadt (Germany), Jamaa (Africa), Fe y alegriá (Latin America), Christophers (U.S.A.), Knights of Columbus (U.S.A. and Europe), JOC and JAC and JEC (France).
23. See Pierre Cren, "The Christian and the World according to Teilhard de Chardin," *Concilium* 19 (1966): 74. "In reading certain theological or spiritual writers it very soon becomes apparent that the side of the equation representing the world is not really present, because it has never really been lived."
24. For further readings in the history of spirituality see: Jean Leclercq, François Vandenbroucke, Louis Bouyer, *A History of Christian Spirituality*, vol. 1 (London: Burns and Oates, 1963), vol. 2 (New York: The Seabury Press, 1968), vol. 3 (New York: The Seabury Press, 1969); also part 1, "Historical Introduction," of A. Auer, *Open to the World*, pp. 21-72.
25. See Ermanno Ancilli, "Orientamenti di spiritualità contemporaneo," *Seminarium* 26 (1974): 203-230.
26. See R. Kevin Seasoltz, "Contemporary American Lay Movements in Spirituality," *Communio* 6 (1979): 339-364.
27. See George Aschenbrenner, "Currents in Spirituality: The Last Decade," *Review for Religious* 39 (1980): 196-218.
28. See especially *Spirituality Today*, vols. 30, 31, 32.
29. Initial insights on these topics were well presented by John XXIII, *Pacem in Terris*, 1963, and Paul VI, *Ecclesiam Suam*, 1964.
30. *Church* here is to be understood less as institution and more as the spirituality of the baptized.
31. See works referred to in note 23 of chap. 1.

32. These are basically the phases of the Council's teaching. References are too numerous to give here, but C 34:2 is the first major ecclesiastical document to formally accept the concept of "consecration of the world."

33. See Matthew Fox, "Introduction: Roots and Routes in Western Spiritual Consciousness," in *Western Spirituality*, pp. 1-18.

34. See, for instance, L'Emery, "L'homme dans l'action politique," in *La Vie Spirituelle* 124 (1971): 311.

35. See Richard J. Mouw, "The Corporate Calling of the Laity," in *The New Laity*, pp. 103-119; also H. Symanowski, *The Christian in an Industrial Society* (London: Collins, 1966), pp. 113 ff; John A. Coleman, "Toward a Church with a Worldly Vocation," in *Challenge to the Laity*, Russell Barta, ed. (Huntington, Indiana: Our Sunday Visitor, Inc., 1980), pp. 75-105.

36. See M. Fox, *A Spirituality Named Compassion* (Minneapolis: Winston Press, 1979), p. ii.

37. For a good explanation of the qualities of a Christian prophet today, see Paul Minear, *To Heal and to Renew* (New York: The Seabury Press, 1976), pp. 87-91. On a closely allied topic, see Dennis Geaney, *The Prophetic Parish: A Center for Peace and Justice* (Minneapolis: Winston Press, 1983).

38. Auer, pp. 334-335.

39. See "The Charter Sermon" in chap. 7 of Doohan, *Luke: The Perennial Spirituality*.

40. See John Paul II, *Rich in Mercy* (Dives in Misericordia).

41. See Juan Capellaro, "Liberi per servire," *Presenza: Quaderni di Spiritualità* 9 (1973): 21-55.

42. Josef Sudbrack, "Spirituality," *Sacramentum Mundi*, vol. 6, p. 149.

43. For additional ideas, see Andrew M. Greeley's *The New Agenda* (New York: Doubleday, 1973).

44. See François Vandenbroucke, "Spirituality and Spiritualities," *Concilium* 9 (1965): 45-60; Hans Urs von Balthasar, "The Gospel as Norm and Test of All Spirituality in the Church," *Concilium* 9 (1965): 7-23.

45. Sudbrack, p. 151.

46. See *1981 Catholic Almanac* (Huntington, Indiana: Our Sunday Visitor, 1980), p. 409.

47. G. Philips, "The Church in the Modern World," *Concilium* 6 (1965): 7.

Concluding Comments

1. Unfortunately, the new Code of Canon Law allows only

consultative voting by laity in all local councils. See Canons 443, 514, and 536. See also Francis Morrissey, "The New Code of Canon Law," *Origins* 11 (1981): 421-430; R. McBrien, "A Theologian's View of the New Code," *Origins* 11 (1981): 430-456.

2. J. B. Metz, "For a Renewed Church Before a New Council: A Concept in Four Theses," in *Toward Vatican III,* David Tracy, Hans Küng, Johannes Metz, eds. (New York: The Seabury Press, 1978), p. 142.

3. Officials of the Church still insist that government, teaching, preaching, and sanctification are institutionalized charisms of the sacrament of orders, and that religious profession leads to a higher ecclesiastical state of perfection. Both ideas are influenced much by historical and sociological developments and have little practical meaning today.

4. U.S. Bishops, "Called and Gifted: Catholic Laity 1980," *Origins* 10 (1980): 370 and 372: "The Call to Ministry."

5. John A. Coleman, "Toward a Church with a Worldly Vocation," in *Challenge to the Laity,* p. 93.

6. "Called and Gifted," p. 372.

7. "Called and Gifted," p. 371.

8. "Called and Gifted," p. 353.

Bibliography

Alfaro, Juan. "Tecnopolis e Cristianesimo." *Civiltà Cattolica* 120 (1969): 533-548.

Allen, Thomas. "Diaconate, Catechumenate, Lay Ministry: Three Elements of a Total Ministry." *To Build and Be Church.* Washington, D.C.: Bishops' Committee on the Laity, 1979, part 1, pp. 24-28.

Ancilli, Ermanno. "Orientamenti di spiritualità contemporaneo." *Seminarium* 26 (1974): 203-230.

Arnau, Ramon. "Lay Participation in Choosing Ministers." *Theology Digest* 28 (1980): 137-141.

Aschenbrenner, George. "Currents in Spirituality, The Past Decade." *Review for Religious* 39 (1980): 196-218.

Auer, Alfons. *Open to the World: An Analysis of Lay Spirituality.* Baltimore: Helicon Press, 1966.

Balthasar, Hans Urs von. "The Gospel as Norm and Test of All Spirituality in the Church." *Concilium* 9 (1965): 7-23.

Bauer, Pam. "Church Not Ready for Lay Ministry." *National Catholic Reporter,* 20 April 1979, pp. 1, 14, 24.

Berdyaev, Nicolas. "Salvation and Creativity: Two Understandings of Christianity." *Western Spirituality.* Matthew Fox, ed. Santa Fe: Bear & Co., 1981, pp. 115-139.

Besnard, Albert-Marie. "Tendencies of Contemporary Spirituality." *Concilium* 9 (1965): 25-44.

Besret, Bernard. *Tomorrow a New Church.* New York: Paulist Press, 1973.

Bonnard, P. "Ministères et laïcat chez Saint Paul." *Verbum Caro* 71/72 (1964): 56-66.

Borders, William, Archbishop of Baltimore. "Collegiality in the Local Church." *Origins* 9 (1980): 509-513.

Bridel, C. "La mission du laïcat." *Verbum Caro* 71/72 (1964): 288-311.

Brown, Robert McAfee. *Frontiers for the Church Today.* New York: Oxford University Press, 1973.

Brugnoli, Pietro. *Missione dei laici nel mondo di oggi.* Brescia, Italy: Morcelliana, 1967.

Brungs, Robert A. *A Priestly People.* New York: Sheed and Ward,

1968.

Bucy, Ralph D., ed. *The New Laity.* Waco, Texas: Word Books, 1978.

Callahan, Daniel. *The Mind of the Catholic Layman.* New York: Scribners, 1963.

Capellaro, Juan. "Liberi per servire." *Presenza: Quaderni di Spiritualità* 9 (1973).

Casey, Juliana. "Maria's Story." *Chicago Studies* 18 (1979): 17-28.

Catherwood, H. F. R. *The Christian in Industrial Society.* London: Tyndale Press, 1964.

Cauwelaert, Jan Van. "The Ordination of the Lay People to Ministries in the Church." *Lumen Vitae* 26 (1971): 585-592.

Charles, P. "Créateur des choses visibles." *Nouvelle Revue Théologique* 67 (1940): 261-279.

Chenu, Marie-Dominique. *The Theology of Work.* Dublin: Gill and Son, 1963.

_____. "I laici e la consecratio mundi." *La Chiesa nel mondo di oggi.* L. G. Barauna, ed. Florence, Italy: Vallecchi Editore, 1966, pp. 978-993.

_____. *Théologie de la matière, civilisation technique et spiritualité chrétienne.* Paris: Editions du Cerf, 1968.

Chicago Declaration of Christian Concern. *National Catholic Reporter,* 20 January 1978, p. 11.

Chicago Declaration of Christian Concern and Responses. *Commonweal* 105 (1978): 108-116.

Code of Canon Law (Latin-English Edition). Washington, D.C.: Canon Law Society of America, 1983.

Cogley, John. "A Good Word for the Marketplace." *The Layman and the Council.* Michael J. Greene, ed. Springfield, Illinois: Templegate, 1964.

Coleman, John A. "Toward a Church with a Worldly Vocation." *Challenge to the Laity.* Russell Barta, ed. Huntington, Indiana: Our Sunday Visitor, Inc., 1980, pp. 75-105.

Comblin, J. "Hacia una teología de la acción." *Annales de la Facultad de Teología de la Universidad de Chile* 14 (1962): 31-98.

Congar, Yves. *Lay People in the Church.* Trans. Donald Attwater. Westminster, Maryland: Newman Press, 1957.

_____. "Ministères et laïcat dans les recherches actuelles de la théologie catholique romaine." *Verbum Caro* 71/72 (1964): 127-148.

_____. *Priest and Layman.* Trans. P. J. Hepburne-Scott. London: Darton, Longman and Todd, 1967.

_____ . "Le role de l'Eglise dans le monde de ce temps." *L'Eglise dans le monde de ce temps*, 2. Paris: Les Editions du Cerf, 1967, pp. 305-328.

_____ . *Ministères et communion ecclesiale*. Paris: Les Editions du Cerf, 1971.

_____ . "What Belonging to the Church Has Come to Mean." *Communio* 4 (1977): 146-160.

Conroy, Donald B. *The Development of a Pastoral Approach to Family Ministry Based on an Emerging Ecclesiology of the Christian Family*. Prepared for Pre-Synod consultation. University of Notre Dame, 1980.

"Consilium de Laicis: Directorium respiciens normas quibus Instituta Internationalia Catholica definiuntur." *Acta Apostolicae Sedis* 63 (1971): 948-956.

Cosgrove, William, Bishop of Belleville. "Resolving Disputes in the Church." *Origins* 11 (1981): 1-8.

Council of European Bishops' Conferences. "The Responsibilities of European Christians." *Origins* 10 (1980): 268-272.

Coudreau, François. "Lay Responsibility in the Church's Theological Mission." *Lumen Vitae* 28 (1973): 609-636.

Cren, Pierre. "The Christian and the World According to Teilhard de Chardin." *Concilium* 19 (1966): 73-87.

Davis, Charles. *God's Grace in History*. London: Fontana, 1967.

DeBoy, James T. "Clergy vs Laity: Must Authority Be Pre-Ordained?" *U.S. Catholic*, September 1980, pp. 32-34.

De Guibert, Joseph. *The Theology of the Spiritual Life*. London: Sheed and Ward, 1965.

de la Potterie, Ignace. "L'origine et le sens primitif du mot 'laïc'." *Nouvelle Revue Théologique* 80 (1958): 840-853.

DeLooz, Pierre. "The Social Function of the Canonization of Saints." *Concilium* 129 (1979): 14-24.

Deloupy, Jean Paul. "Promotion du laïcat et sacerdoce." *Nouvelle Revue Théologique* 100 (1978): 20-35.

de Margerie, B. "Le Christ, la sécularisation et la consécration du monde." *Nouvelle Revue Théologique* 91 (1969): 370-395.

De Sales, Francis. *Introduction to the Devout Life*. London: Burns and Oates, 1962.

De Smedt, Emile Joseph, Bishop of Bruges. *The Priesthood of the Faithful*. New York: Paulist Press, 1962.

_____ . "Priesthood of All the Faithful." *Council Speeches of Vatican II*. Yves Congar, Hans Küng, Daniel O'Hanlon, eds. New York: Sheed and Ward, 1964, pp. 25-28.

_____. "Il sacerdozio dei fedeli." *La Chiesa del Vaticano II*. L. G. Barauna, ed. Florence, Italy: Vallecchi Editore, 1965, pp. 453-464.

Dixon, Robert C., and Dean R. Hoge. "Models and Priorities of the Catholic Church as Held by Suburban Laity." *Review of Religious Research* 20 (1979): 150-167.

Dondeyne, Albert. *La Fede in Ascolto del Mondo*. Assisi: Cittadella Editrice, 1966.

Doohan, Leonard. *Luke: The Perennial Spirituality*. Santa Fe: Bear and Co., 1982.

Dubarle, Dominique. "L'Eglise et le monde: harmonie ou divorce?" *Vie Spirituelle* 78 (1948): 311-335, 613-637.

Dulles, Avery. *Models of the Church*. New York: Doubleday and Co., Inc., 1974.

_____. *The Resilient Church*. New York: Doubleday and Co., Inc., 1977.

_____. "Imaging the Church for the 1980s." *Thought* 56 (1981): 121-138.

Duquoc, Christian. "Signification ecclesiale du laïcat." *Lumière et Vie* 65 (1963): 73-98.

Dyckman, Catherine, and L. Patrick Carroll. *Inviting the Mystic, Supporting the Prophet*. New York: Paulist Press, 1981.

Eagleson, John, and Philip Scharper, eds. *Puebla and Beyond*. New York: Orbis Books, 1979.

Early Christian Writings. Harmondsworth, England: Penguin Books, 1968.

Elsesser, Suzanne. "Full-Time Lay Ministers in the Church." *Origins* 10 (1980): 145-151.

Ernst, Josef. "The Significance of Christ's Eucharistic Body for the Unity of the Church and Cosmos." *Concilium* 40 (1968): 106-116.

Finley, Mitch, and Kathy Finley. "Family." *Modern Ministries*, May-November issues, 1981.

Flick, Maurizio. "Costruttori del mondo e pellegrini nel mondo." *Civiltà Cattolica* 116 (1965): 218-221.

_____. "Riflessioni metodologiche per una teologia del progresso." *Civiltà Cattolica* 120 (1969): 119-128.

Fox, Matthew. *A Spirituality Named Compassion*. Minneapolis: Winston Press, 1979.

_____. "Introduction: Roots and Routes in Western Spiritual Consciousness." *Western Spirituality*. Santa Fe: Bear and Co., 1981, pp. 1-24.

Geaney, Dennis. *Emerging Lay Ministries*. Kansas City: Andrews and McMeel, Inc., 1979.

──────── . *The Prophetic Parish: A Center for Peace and Justice*. Minneapolis: Winston Press, 1983.

Gerety, Peter, Archbishop of Newark. "Women in the Church." *Origins* 10 (1981): 582-588.

Gibbs, John G. "Pauline Cosmic Christology and Ecological Crisis." *Journal of Biblical Literature* 90 (1971): 466-479.

Gilkey, Langdon. *Catholicism Confronts Modernity*. New York: The Seabury Press, 1975.

Gillespie, Thomas W. "The Laity in Biblical Perspective." *Theology Today* 36 (1979-80): 315-327.

Gognet, Louis. *Post-Reformation Spirituality*. New York: Hawthorn Books, 1959.

Gonzalez Ruiz, José-Marie. "A Spirituality for a Time of Uncertainty." *Concilium* 19 (1966): 59-72.

Greeley, Andrew M. *The New Agenda*. New York: Doubleday and Co., Inc., 1973.

Guitton, Jean. *The Church and the Laity*. New York: Alba House, 1965.

Gutierrez, Gustavo. "Notes for a Theology of Liberation." *Theological Studies* 31 (1970): 244-261.

Haight, Roger D. "Mission: The Symbol for Understanding the Church Today." *Theological Studies* 37 (1976): 620-649.

Hamer, Jerome. "The Lay Apostolate as a State of Life." *The Church Is a Communion*. New York: Sheed and Ward, 1964, pp. 142-155.

Häring, Bernard. *A Theology of Protest*. New York: Farrar, Straus, and Giroux, 1970.

Hemrick, Eugene. "The Need to Define Roles." *Origins* 10 (1980): 151-154.

Hubbard, Howard J., Bishop of Albany. "We Are His People: A Pastoral Letter." *To Build and Be Church*. Washington, D.C.: Bishops' Committee on the Laity, 1979, part 1, pp. 9-19.

Jessup, H. "Ex-extraordinary Minister, Priest at Odds Over Her Parish Duties." *National Catholic Reporter*, 20 May 1977, p. 3.

──────── . "90 Forgotten of Boston Try Action For Recognition." *National Catholic Reporter*, 28 January 1977, p. 3.

John Paul II, Pope. "Redemptor Hominis." *Origins* 8 (1979): 625-644.

──────── . "Opening Homily for the Synod on the Family." *Origins* 10 (1980): 257-260.

──────── . "The Role of the Laity in Africa." *Origins* 10 (1980):

-161-

47-48.

_____. "Address to Lay Church Workers." *Origins* 10 (1980): 390-394.

_____. "Apostolic Exhortation on the Family." *Origins* 11 (1981): 437-468.

Jones, Arthur. "Bishops: Laity Invisible to the World." *National Catholic Reporter*, 30 March 1979, pp. 12-16.

Kaam, Adrian Van. *In Search of Spiritual Identity*. Denville, New Jersey: Dimension Books, 1975.

Kelly, H. "The Asceticism of the Modern Apostolate." *Doctrine and Life* (1967), pp. 357-358.

Kelly, William. "Reflections on the Status of a Theology of the Layman." *Theological Studies* 28 (1967): 706-732.

Kinast, Robert. "The Laity, A Theological Perspective." *To Build and Be Church*. Washington, D.C.: Bishops' Committee on the Laity, 1979, part 1, pp. 5-8.

Küng, Hans. *The Church*. New York: Sheed and Ward, 1967.

_____. "Participation of the Laity in Church Leadership and in Church Elections." *Journal of Ecumenical Studies* 6 (1969): 511-533.

Lally, Patrick. "NAL or Never for Laity." *Commonweal* 86 (1967): 437-438.

Larkin, Ernest E. *Spiritual Renewal of the American Priesthood*. Washington, D.C.: USCC, 1973.

Leckey, Dolores R. "Looking at Lay Ministry: Historically, Practically, Theologically." *To Build and Be Church*. Washington, D.C.: Bishops' Committee on the Laity, 1979, part 2, pp. 13-16.

Leclercq, Jean, François Vandenbroucke, and Louis Bouyer. *A History of Christian Spirituality*, vol. 1. London: Burns and Oates, 1963; vol. 2. New York: The Seabury Press, 1968; vol. 3. New York: The Seabury Press, 1969.

Lee, Bernard. *The Becoming of the Church*. New York: Paulist Press, 1974.

L'Emery, Louis. "Expérience de la foi dans l'action politique." *La Vie Spirituelle* 124 (1971): 295-311.

Lynch, Thomas J. "Labor Unions in Catholic Institutions." *Origins* 10 (1980): 363-365.

Lyonnet, Stanislas. "La rédemption de l'univers." *Lumière et Vie* 48 (1960): 43-62.

Margaret, Teresa. "Prayer in the Secular City." *Spiritual Life* 19 (1968): 72-84.

McBrien, Richard P. "A Theology of the Laity." *American*

Ecclesiastical Review 160 (1969): 73-86.

—————. "Church." *Chicago Studies* 12 (1973): 241-255.

—————. *The Remaking of the Church, An Agenda for Reform*. New York: Harper and Row, 1973.

—————. "Call to Action Reflects the People of God Image." *National Catholic Reporter*, 12 November 1976, p. 20.

—————. "A Theologian's View of the New Code." *Origins* 11 (1981): 430-456.

McCarthy, Timothy. *The Postconciliar Christian: The Meaning of the Priesthood of Laity*. New York: Kenedy, 1967.

McCormick, Richard A. "The Magisterium: A New Model." *America*, 27 June 1970, pp. 674-676.

Message of the Canadian Bishops: Charismatic Renewal. Ottawa: Publication Service, Canadian Catholic Conference, 1975.

Mesthene, Emmanuel. "Religious Values in the Age of Technology." *Concilium* 36 (1967): 109-124.

Metz, Johannes B. *Theology of the World*. New York: Herder and Herder, 1969.

—————. "For A Renewed Church Before A New Council: A Concept in Four Theses." *Towards Vatican III*. David Tracy, Hans Küng, and Johannes B. Metz, eds. New York: The Seabury Press, 1978, pp. 137-145.

Minear, Paul. *To Heal and to Renew*. New York: The Seabury Press, 1976.

Molette, Charles. "Brève Histoire de l'Action Catholique." *Lumière et Vie* 63 (1963): 45-82.

Morawska, Anna. "Introduction to a Theology for Laymen." *Cross Currents* 17 (1967): 5-14.

Morrissey, Francis. "The New Code of Canon Law." *Origins* 11 (1981): 421-430.

Moreira Nevas, Lucas. "A Layperson in a Vast World." *Osservatore Romano* (Eng. ed.), 1 September 1977, p. 8.

Mouw, Richard J. "The Corporate Calling of the Laity." *The New Laity*. Ralph D. Bucy, ed. Waco, Texas: Word Books, 1978, pp. 103-119.

Muhlen, Heribert. *Una Mistica Persona*. Rome: Città Nuova Editrice, 1968.

Mulders, Jacques. "After the Dutch Synod." *The Month* 13 (1980): 189-194.

Nicodemus, Donald E. *The Democratic Church*. Milwaukee: The Bruce Publishing Co., 1968.

Nicolas, J. H. "Les laïcs et l'annonce de la parole de Dieu." *Nouvelle*

Revue Théologique 93 (1971): 821-848.

Niedergeses, James, Bishop of Nashville, Tenn. "Governing A Local Church." *Origins* 9 (1980): 637-641.

O'Boyle, Patrick A., Archbishop of Washington, D.C. "The Spirituality of the Social Apostolate." *Catholic Mind* 65 (1967): 37-41.

O'Brien, David. *The Renewal of American Catholicism.* New York: Oxford University Press, 1972.

_____ . "The Ministerial Church: Realism and Responsibility." *Chicago Studies* 16 (1977): 167-194.

O'Grady, Desmond. "Laity Out, Clerics In." *National Catholic Reporter,* 7 January 1977, p. 2.

Panteghini, Gabriele. *Il mondo materiale nel piano della salvezza.* Rome: Edizioni Pauline, 1968.

Paul VI, Pope. *On the Development of Peoples.* Populorum Progressio. 1967.

_____ . "Allocutio iis qui interfuerunt Conventui tertio de apostolatu laicorum ex omnibus nationibus Romae habito." *Acta Apostolicae Sedis* 59 (1967): 1040-1048.

_____ . "Allocutio Moderatoribus ac Membris e Consilio de Laicis qui octavo plenario Coetui Romae habito interfuerunt." *Acta Apostolicae Sedis* 62 (1970): 213-216.

Philips, Gérard. *The Role of the Laity in the Church.* Notre Dame, Indiana: Fides, 1955.

_____ . "The Church in the Modern World." *Concilium* 6 (1965): 5-22.

_____ . *Achieving Christian Maturity.* Chicago: Franciscan Herald Press, 1966.

Rahner, Karl. "L'apostolat des laïcs." *Nouvelle Revue Théologique* 78 (1956): 3-32.

_____ . "The Order of Redemption within the Order of Creation." *Mission and Grace,* vol. 1. New York: Sheed and Ward, 1963, pp. 59-113.

_____ . "The Theological Interpretation of the Position of Christians in the Modern World." *Mission and Grace,* vol. 1. New York: Sheed and Ward, 1963, pp. 3-55.

_____ . *Christian in the Marketplace.* New York: Sheed and Ward, 1966.

_____ . "Democracy in the Church?" *The Month* 39 (1968): 105-119.

_____ . "Sacramental Basis for the Role of the Layman in the Church." *Theological Investigations,* 8. New York: Herder and Herder, 1971.

_____. *The Shape of the Church to Come.* New York: The Seabury Press, 1972.

_____. "Open Letter to Cardinal Ratzinger." *National Catholic Reporter,* 23 November 1979, p. 1.

Reegan, Otto Ter. "The Rights of the Laity." *Concilium* 38 (1968): 17-30.

Remy, J. "Fault and Guilt in the Perspective of Sociology." *Concilium* 61 (1971): 10-25.

Riedlinger, Helmut. "How Universal Is Christ's Kingship?" *Concilium* 11 (1966): 107-127.

Ruether, Rosemary. "Matters Left Unsaid." *Commonweal* 105 (1978): 112-113.

Sanks, H., and B. Smith, "Liberation Ecclesiology: Praxis, Theory, Praxis." *Theological Studies* 38 (1977): 3-38.

Schillebeeckx, Edward. *The Layman in the Church.* New York: St. Paul Publications, 1963.

_____. "Definizione del laico cristiano." *La Chiesa del Vaticano II.* L. G. Barauna, ed. Florence, Italy: Vallecchi Editore. 1965, pp. 959-977.

_____, ed. "The Church and Mankind." *Concilium* 1 (1965).

_____. "A New Type of Layman." *Spiritual Life* 14 (1968): 14-24.

_____. *God the Future of Man.* New York: Sheed and Ward, 1969.

_____. "The Catholic Understanding of Office in the Church." *Theological Studies* 69 (1969): 567-587.

Sears, Robert T. "Trinitarian Love as Ground of the Church." *Theological Studies* 37 (1976): 652-679.

Seasoltz, R. Kevin. "Contemporary American Lay Movements in Spirituality." *Communio* 6 (1979): 339-364.

Speigl, Jakob. "Lay Participation in Early Church Councils." *Theology Digest* 28 (1980): 141-142.

Steindl-Rast, David. "The Environment as Guru." *Cross Currents* 24 (1974): 148-153.

Stewart, Richard L. "Et renovabis faciem terrae." *Clergy Review* 49 (1964): 593-604.

Sudbrack, Josef. "Spirituality." *Sacramentum Mundi,* vol. 6. Karl Rahner, ed. New York: Herder and Herder, 1970, pp. 147-153.

Symanowski, Horst. *The Christian Witness in an Industrial Society.* London: Collins, 1966.

Tavard, George A. "Is There a Catholic Ecclesiology?" *Catholic Theological Society of America, Proceedings.* 1974, pp. 367-380.

Thils, Gustave. *La théologie des realités terrestres*. Bruges: De Brouwer, 1946.

_____ . "L'activité humaine dans l'univers." *L'Eglise dans le monde de ce temps*, II. Paris: Les Editions du Cerf, 1967, pp. 279-303.

Thomas, David M. *The Prophetic Role of the Christian Family: A Proposal for the Foundational Church.* Prepared for Pre-Synod Consultation, University of Notre Dame, 1980.

Thorman, Donald. *The Emerging Layman: The Role of the Catholic Layman in America.* New York: Doubleday and Co., Inc., 1957.

Tillard, Jean-Marie R. "La Chiesa e i valori terrestri." *La Chiesa nel mondo di oggi.* L. G. Barauna, ed. Florence, Italy: Vallecchi Editore, 1966, pp. 213-250.

Tremel, Y. B. "L'Eglise dans le monde." *Lumière et Vie* 65 (1963): 22-36.

Truhlar, Karel V. "Transformatio mundi et fuga mundi." *Gregorianum* 38 (1957): 406-445.

_____ . "The Earthly Cast of the Beatitudes." *Concilium* 39 (1968): 33-43.

U.S. Bishops. "Called and Gifted: Catholic Laity 1980." *Origins* 10 (1980): 369-373.

U.S. Bishops' Committee on the Laity. *To Build and Be Church.* Washington, D.C., 1979.

U.S. Bishops' Committee on the Parish. "The Parish: A People, A Mission, A Structure." *Origins* 10 (1981): 641-646.

U.S. Bishops' National Advisory Council. "The Thrust of Lay Ministry." *Origins* 9 (1980): 621-626.

Uylenbroeck, Marcel, Mons. "Lay Associations in the Church." *Osservatore Romano* (English ed.), 18 August 1977, p. 8.

Vandenbroucke, François. "Spirituality and Spiritualities." *Concilium* 9 (1965): 45-60.

Walsh, James. "Theology of Obedience." *Way Supplement* 5 (1968).

Walsh, Michael. "Second-Class Citizens of the Kingdom." *The Month* 4 (1971): 142-144.

Warnach, V. "Symbol and Reality in the Eucharist." *Concilium* 40 (1969): 82-105.

Williams, Margaret. "Apostolic Contemplation." *Way Supplement* 7 (1969): 97-103.

Index of Subjects

This index should be used in conjunction with the detailed Table of Contents.

A

Authority, 7, 17, 30, 32, 37, 42, 45, 49, 55, 89, 128

B

Baptism, 10, 11, 17, 18, 24, 71, 72, 73, 79, 82, 85, 86, 87, 97, 101, 112, 133
  baptismal responsibilities, 2, 12, 19, 24, 25, 43, 47, 82, 86, 112
  baptismal rights, 18, 26, 34, 35, 44, 46, 86, 133
Basic ecclesial communities, 18, 39, 88, 105
Bishops, 17, 18, 31, 47
Burnout in lay ministers, 52

C

Catholic Action, 5
Charisms, 11, 17, 28, 44, 45, 48, 86, 96, 101, 102, 114, 130
Charity, 86, 102, 115
Chicago Declaration of Christian Concern, 1
Christology, 13
Church (*see* Models)
Clericalization, 7, 59, 103
Code of Canon Law, 4, 6, 30, 31, 36
Collaboration, 36, 37, 50, 129
Collegiality, 7, 35
Community, 22, 40, 44, 74, 87, 89, 104, 133
Confirmation, 17, 101
Conscience, 33, 113, 131, 132
Contestation, 36, 55, 110
Conversion, 15, 39, 44, 63, 98, 105, 113
Coresponsibility, 26, 27, 31, 33, 36, 38, 47, 86, 87, 101, 105, 124, 131
Councils, 87
  pastoral, 18, 31, 38,

Jurisdiction, 30, 48

K

Kingdom, 14

L

Lay apostolate
(see also Ministry,
lay), 2, 3, 8
Lay ministries, 6, 31
Leadership, 39, 42, 45,
57, 63, 90, 130, 131,
134
Liberation theology, 1,
14
Liberty, 7, 34, 43, 47, 86
Liturgy, 12, 16, 18, 28,
39, 41, 43, 87, 102,
106, 107, 114

M

Magisterium of the
Church, 7
Mandate, 5, 6, 18, 48,
57
Marriage, 10, 30, 41, 75,
93
education of children,
76
family ministry, 44
sexual life, 12, 41, 42
Ministries, 19, 48, 86,
87, 109
Church finance, 2, 52
ecumenism, 2
education, 2, 19, 48
evangelization, 19, 44,
109, 131
family, 44, 45, 83
liturgical, 19
non-ecclesiastically
controlled, 49
parish life, 2
prophetical, 14, 21,
33, 54, 111, 130
team, 19, 48
world transformation,
13, 15, 16, 44, 50,
109
Ministry
lay, 10, 19, 26, 27, 32,
43, 44, 45, 48,
50, 53
auxiliary to
hierarchy, 6, 11
commitment to, xi
facilitating, 3, 46,
47
importance of, xi,
18, 81
intervocational, 19,
22, 48, 109, 118,
133
priestly, xi, 20
Mission
of Church, xii, 5, 6, 7,
8, 17, 24, 35, 44,
47, 79, 86, 128,
129, 133
of hierarchy, 5, 25, 48

-169-

R

S

T

12, 13
Theologies of laity
(*see* Models of
Church), 6, 129
Theology
of laity, 3, 16, 20, 22,
25
training for laity, xiii,
38, 52, 114
Third World Congress
on Lay Apostolate,
2

U

Universal call to
holiness, 42, 94,
100, 102, 129, 131
U.S. bishops, 46, 50, 52,
135

V

Vocation, 56, 86, 93,
112, 113

W

Work, 9, 10, 11, 43
World, 10, 12, 13, 24, 41,
107, 124, 132
"flight from," 11, 95,
101
involvement, 10, 20,
41, 86, 103, 124
value in spirituality, 8,

9, 11, 14, 107

Index of Personal Names

A

Ancilli, Ermanno, 104
Aquinas, Thomas, 98
Aschenbrenner, George,
104
Augustine, 41, 69, 71

B

Bérulle, Cardinal
de, 100
Besnard, Albert-
Marie, 91
Brown, Robert
McAfee, 54

C

Charlemagne, 97
Chenu, Marie-
Dominique, 8
Congar, Yves, 8, 9, 12,
16, 24
Cosgrove, Bishop
William, 34

D

Day, Dorothy, 101

Dominic, 121
Duff, Frank, 101
Dulles, Avery, 64, 65, 66,
88
Duquoc, Christian, 8

E

Elsesser, Suzanne, 51, 52
Erasmus of Rotterdam,
98

F

Fox, Matthew, 107
Francis of Assisi, 121
Francis of Sales, 99, 100

G

Gregory the Great, 96
Gregory VII, 97
Gregory of Nyssa, 117

H

Häring, Bernard, 97
Hügel, Friedrich von,
101

I

Ignatius of Loyola, 99,
121

J

John of the Cross, 99,
121
John XXIII, 5, 62, 63
John Paul I, 62, 63
John Paul II, 15, 37, 42,
46, 49

K

Kempis, Thomas à, 98
Kinast, Robert, 46
Küng, Hans, 29

L

Leo XIII, 64
Lynch, Thomas J., 52,
55

M

Maritain, Jacques, 101
May, Bishop John L., 50
McBrien, Richard P., 3,
8, 17
Metz, Johannes B., 131

More, Thomas, 98

N

Niedergeses, Bishop
James, 33

O

O'Brien, David, 37

P

Paul VI, 3, 5, 6, 7, 30,
62, 63
Philips, Gérard, 7, 12,
20
Pius XI, 5
Pius XII, 5

R

Rahner, Karl, 9, 12, 17,
32, 33
Ratzinger, Cardinal
Joseph, 33

S

Schillebeeckx, Edward,
8, 9, 12, 23, 56
Seasoltz, R. Kevin, 104
Sheed, Frank, 101